A
Sponsorship
Guide
for 12-Step
Programs

A Sponsorship Guide for 12-Step Programs

by M.T.

ST. MARTIN'S GRIFFIN ✒ NEW YORK

A SPONSORSHIP GUIDE FOR TWELVE-STEP PROGRAMS. Copyright © 1995, 1998 by M. T. All rights reserved.

Printed in the United States of America. For information, address St. Martin's Press, 175 Fifth Avenue, New York, N.Y. 10010

DESIGN BY BARBARA M. BACHMAN

Library of Congress Cataloging-in-Publication Data

M. T., 1950–

   A sponsorship guide for twelve-step programs : advice for recovery-related problems / M. T.—1st St. Martin's Griffin ed.

   p. cm.

   Rev. ed. of: A sponsorship guide for all twelve-step programs.

West Palm Beach, FL : PT Publications, 1995.

   Includes bibliographical references (p.).

   ISBN 0-312-18182-5

   1. Twelve-step programs. 2. Recovering addicts. I. M. T., 1950–. Sponsorship guide for all twelve-step programs. II. Title.

HV4998.M2   1998

   616.86'106—dc21

97-47262

CIP

D 10 9 8 7

In memory of

RONNIE C.

(A.K.A. AA SALAHUDDIN)

He gave freely of what he had,

and was an inspiration to

all who knew him.

I owe many thanks to

PATRICE S.

Without her love, guidance, and support,

this book would not have been possible.

Contents

SPONSORSHIP BASICS

1. In the Beginning *1*

   *What makes a good sponsor? Some suggestions to
   give a newcomer who has asked you to sponsor him/
   her. The most important things our participants said
   they were told by their sponsors.*

2. Gender Issues 25

   *Should you agree to sponsor someone of the opposite
   sex? Some thoughts on gay sponsorship: Is same sex/
   sexual preference sponsorship a problem? Are there
   special considerations for taking on a sponsee who is
   HIV+?*

3. Sponsor/Sponsee Relationships 43

   *Is it necessary or important to develop a friendship
   (i.e., socialize) with your sponsee or just be there to
   give direction with the steps and working the
   program? What is fair for sponsors to expect from
   their sponsees?*

WORKING THE STEPS
WITH A SPONSEE

*Should you start with the First Step regardless of
how many steps your sponsee may have already
worked? To write or not to write? Do you work the
steps the same way with each sponsee? How can you
help sponsees with their understanding of a higher
power?*

*How do you gauge when it's time for a sponsee to
write his/her Fourth Step? What direction can you
give? What is your part, as a sponsor, in doing a
Fifth Step?*

What direction can you give in working these steps?

*Some suggestions for working the amends steps.
What to suggest to a sponsee with outstanding legal
problems?*

SOME COMMON ISSUES THAT COME UP AND WHAT TO DO WHEN THEY ARISE

IN CONCLUSION

Preface

Below is the forward that appeared in the first edition of this book. This is a new edition with a new publisher, St. Martin's Press. I am very happy that they are now publishing this book—this new edition looks terrific, and I've had the opportunity to do some more work on it. Also, it is now available at a more affordable price. Even at the higher price, thousands of copies of the first edition were sold, and the feedback was very rewarding. This book has apparently helped many people work with others. I hope you and those you work with will benefit from the information given here, and that it will help you to become a better sponsor or sponsee!

Why a book on sponsorship?

A little while ago, I was wishing for a "learning day" on sponsorship. How nice it would be, I thought, to ask questions of other sponsors—as a group—and learn from their experiences. It seemed to me that my experiences were probably being duplicated every day, yet I didn't have access to all of those results (as we often do with so many other topics of recovery that are shared at meetings). Rather than reinventing the wheel with every situation new to me, I thought it would be much easier, and more beneficial, to learn from others who had been there before me.

When I told this to Patrice, my sponsor, she agreed. After some thought, she suggested that I write a book, because she figured there were many people going through the same things who could use the information.

The process started by developing a questionnaire, then interviewing people whose recovery I admired and who I knew were experienced sponsors. Altogether, seventeen sponsors were interviewed for this book. Patrice and I have also included our own experiences at twenty-three and nine years (respectively) clean and sober. The sponsors interviewed are from different parts of the country (see the following list of acknowledgments) and have different lengths of recovery (some only a few years, some a few decades), together having more than 225 years and having sponsored nearly 600 people! They are African-American, Caucasian, white, male, female, gay, lesbian, addicts, and alcoholics. Many other fellowships are represented, as the steps are the same in each of the many fellowships available today and, in most cases, so are the suggestions given to sponsees. I feel that issues covered in this book will be of use to anyone in any fellowship dealing with sponsorship issues.

As you read, you will see that everyone has their own way of passing on the program to others. I am not presenting any one idea as more valid than the other, and the order is random—I just wanted the book to flow and to show contrasts among people who all have good recoveries. One person can make a good case for one thing, and another can make an equally good case for the exact opposite. So, keep an open mind. What doesn't sound like an option with your sponsee now might be right for another situation a year from now.

I wrote this book as a service. There are so many books and pamphlets on the steps, and so little on this all-important aspect of the recovery process. In meetings we share the most intimate details of our lives, but it is the rare share that talks about sponsorship in any detail. Yet we all deal with the issues of sponsorship: Either we have a sponsor or we are a sponsor—or both! But not every person has a great sponsor (this book is for you) and even if they do, there are bound to be situations that come up that are not in their own or their sponsor's experience (this book is for both of you). And even if a sponsor has experience with an issue, their approach may not be the best for the situation at hand. Realizing that, the sponsor may not know what to suggest (this book is also for you). I've found that it's tough enough to know what direction to take with your own life, let alone to direct someone else's—even if you have some objectivity about it. This book is meant as a resource for those new situations and for new ideas to old situations.

I hope the wisdom of the years of experience contained herein will help you to be a better sponsor. Perhaps the various experiences will confirm what you think is the right action to take or show you other alternatives and ideas for a given situation.

Does this book answer every question about sponsorship? Of course not. This book is not meant to be the last word on the subject, but the first. I hope you get as much out of reading this book as I have in writing it.

With much love and the wish for success in all your endeavors in recovery,

M.T.

Acknowledgments

In the various fellowships we learn that if we turn over our will, things will just "come." Our Higher Power will put in our path the things we need. This was precisely the case with this book coming together. What I had not realized during the five years I worked freelance in my field, travelling the U.S. and staying in other cities for up to two months at a time, was that the many people I met, whose company and recovery I enjoyed, would also be the resources for this book.

I very much wanted to include some step worksheets and was really impressed with the simplicity and thoroughness of "Writing the Steps" generously donated by Ed of New York City. They have sustained only the most minor changes and additions.

I wish to thank Jeanne Gamba for her meticulous transcribing, and the following sponsors who appear in this book for their time and participation in this project:

BOB B.—Los Angeles, California—thirty-two years (has sponsored more than a hundred)

LISA C.—Plantation, Florida—eleven-and-a-half years (has sponsored thirty)

MARIASHA—Santa Monica, California—fourteen years (has sponsored twenty-five)

BEA S.—Van Nuys, California—eight-and-a-half years (has sponsored fifty)

J. P.—Staten Island, New York—six years (has sponsored twelve)

JEANETTE A.—Los Angeles, California—thirty-two years (has sponsored more than sixty)

DON—Los Angeles, California—fifteen-and-a-half years (has sponsored a hundred)

MARGE M.—Los Angeles, California—fifteen years (has sponsored fifty)

LEIGH G.—Los Angeles, California—ten years (has sponsored thirty-eight)

NATALIE C.—Las Vegas, Nevada—ten years (has sponsored thirteen)

KAREN W.—Los Angeles, California—four-and-a-half years (has sponsored six)

LOIS Z.—Carson City, Nevada—fourteen-and-a-half years (has sponsored thirty)

DANNY M.—Culver City, California—four-and-a-half years (has sponsored ten)

SUNNY S.—Las Vegas, Nevada—nine years (has sponsored thirty)

SUZANNE—Los Angeles, California—thirteen years (has sponsored three)

CHARLES H. J.—Los Angeles, California—ten years (has sponsored thirty-five)

ED—New York City, New York—seven years (has sponsored fifteen)

A
Sponsorship
Guide
for 12-Step
Programs

Chapter One

In the Beginning

"*I tell [my sponsees] not to compare
their recovery to anyone else's;
I can only compare me to me.*"

— LISA

What makes a good sponsor? Some suggestions to give a newcomer who has asked you to sponsor them. The most important things told to our sponsors by their sponsors.

There is a common belief that a strong foundation is instrumental to long-term recovery. What newcomers do in their first ninety days and in their first months with a sponsor are key to how they will work the rest of their program. During this formative time, what basic things can you have your sponsees do to set this foundation and establish your relationship with them? Below are some suggestions. Quite honestly, I believed that our sponsor participants, especially on a question as basic as this one, would have pretty much the same answers. I was quite surprised to find out otherwise. It is consistent throughout this book that the answers are inconsistent. Everyone has an individual approach, and it's a plus to have so many perspectives to choose from. You may not choose to do what they did, but what they did may help you choose what to do.

WHAT MAKES A GOOD SPONSOR?

M.T.: I think a good sponsor is someone who has worked the steps, has a strong program, and is passionate and inspired about her recovery.

CHARLES: I think a great sponsor is one who is available whenever possible, one who always reminds us of who we are and why we're doing what we're doing. In other words, our biggest problem is we forget. I recently (in the past three years) moved away from somebody I loved very much, and then got back with that person and continued the relationship. My sponsor reminded me of why I moved out. I'm ten years sober, and I moved out at seven years sober. Moving out was one of the best things I ever did. I forgot why I moved out, and after he asked me the question three times, I remembered why. But I had to hear the question asked three times. I consider myself a pretty good listener. So, for all of us, not just for my own experience, our biggest problem is we forget.

That's what Bob and Bill did for each other. They didn't talk to each other; they listened to each other.

I don't like "don'ts." I like "dos." I think "don'ts" have a way of being self-defeating. I'd like to see: "This is what we do." I'd like to see that over and over again. "This is what we do to stay sober." I don't want to hear anything about, "We don't do that." That's crap. We do everything. So I think, if we get into what we do to stay sober, that's where the emphasis should be.

My responsibility as your sponsor is for you to see that I love you, that the only purpose I have in life is to be loving to you, and, in that sense, loving to myself. As your sponsor, I also try to get you to see (no matter how big, mean and tough or nasty you are or how many things you've gone through) that your parents aren't responsible for your actions, even if your family was dysfunctional. You are responsible for your own actions. And, again, I'm here to love you and to be loved. That's the key to the program.

SUZANNE: I think it's the same thing that makes a really good person: to be a good sponsor, you have to live what you're teaching. I don't think it works to tell people what to do if you're not doing it yourself. It's really easy to boss people around, give them direction, and act like you're a know-it-all. It's much more difficult to live and practice these principles in all of our affairs. I think if that's what you're doing in your life, than you're going to be a good sponsor, because you're an example. That's what this program is, a program of attraction, not promotion, to share my experience, strength, and hope for fun and for free.

Being a sponsor doesn't mean you have to know everything. It means you're just down the road, a few steps ahead of the person behind you. If you don't know, there are lots of other people you can ask. It's like a mentoring program, more than anything else, not like being someone's mother, father, baby-sitter, boss, or caretaker. It's a loving extension of your knowledge, your experience, your strength, and your hope. You do it for fun and for free. If you're not having fun doing it, there's something wrong with your attitude and your approach. I really have a problem with this party line in a lot of AA meetings: if you don't go to meetings all the time, you're going to die, if you don't get a sponsor, you're going to drink and die—a kind of fear-driven focus to go to meetings and have a sponsor. I know a lot of people who are sober who don't go to AA and don't have a sponsor. I think people can stay sober and work the steps by being involved in the fellowship and by participating. I don't think you get the degree and the depth of sobriety without working with someone, because someone doesn't get to know you intimately. I have friends on the East Coast who have been sober for many, many years, and they've never written a Fourth Step. I also feel they don't have the same kind of serenity and spiritual connectedness as people who I know who have written a Fourth Step. The *Big Book* doesn't say you have to have a sponsor, it's not written anywhere. But it is written that we help another alcoholic. So, I think in all of our relationships with people in meetings, we're really sponsoring anyone we have a conversation with. There may just be somebody who we're more particularly connected to in sponsoring.

MARGE: Someone who's willing to share all of her experience, strength, and hope, not just the fluffy parts; someone who is willing to try to pursue her spiritual search so that she is the best human being that she can be at any given time. And someone who's willing to put aside her stuff to direct her attention to someone else. Sometimes that requires a lot of willingness.

MARIASHA: Sponsorship means different things to different people. Do they need to be controlled? Do they need to be told what to do, when to do it, and how to do it? No. Do we need ongoing love and support in our recovery? Yes. I think we could all benefit from having a mentor or a partner to walk the path with and just check in with and touch base with. When you're in isolation, recovery is measured by the degree you participate in it. To think you've arrived and no longer need to check out reality with another human being is a dangerous position to take.

I've chosen to sign up for the long run because of what I receive as a result of that surrender. I've never been totally comfortable with labeling myself. But that is partially why it took me two years to find a sponsor. When I first was clean, I was about to be married, I was in a committed relationship, I had just been accepted into graduate school, and I had never been arrested. I had good relations with my family. I had never written a bad check. I'd never been evicted. I was not a "curb creature," as I heard talked about in a meeting. I was pretty much an upstanding member of society. When I looked around the room, there weren't too many people who fit that bill. There wasn't a lot of clean time in this area; there was very little. I can count on one hand the people who had as much or more time than I had in this area. What was suggested to me (I think it was one of the most valuable things I ever heard) was try to find somebody whose life seems to be improved as a result of working the Twelve Steps of NA who can teach me about working the steps. It doesn't matter what she looks like, what her sexuality is, what her experience has been, what her religion is, or what her familial status is. What matters is, Is she staying clean and does she work the Twelve Steps of NA? Choose somebody based upon those criteria and let go of the other stuff. I picked a sponsor who was as opposite from me as you could probably imagine. But she was working the Twelve Steps, and she was of service and still is today. She has not relapsed; she doesn't relate to some of the experiences I've had, but she relates to the feelings. She always relates to me on a "feel" level. That's my biggest suggestion: if you're looking for a sponsor, try not to think twice about the criteria you're using to make that selection. Do you respect her and see her as knowledgeable? Do you speak the language of the heart with one another? Do you feel she is a positive role model? That is what your decision should be based upon. Not how similar you are in terms of status symbols.

BEA: I don't know what a good sponsor is. What does that mean, "a really good sponsor?" Sponsors are good because they're there for you in your life, and even if they're not there the way you want them to be, you get something out of it, you still learn something. I don't like this idea of firing sponsors. I don't like that lingo. If someone takes the time to care about you, that's very special.

DANNY: I think the most basic thing that makes a really good sponsor is caring. If somebody comes into this program and connects with someone who cares, then he'll start to care about himself. I think that's one of things that's so intimidating about asking someone to sponsor you. When somebody asks you, it's like, "Wow!" "Why?" and "Thank you!" at the same time. Most of the people I sponsor have approached me at meetings I go to regularly where they have heard me share. I think it's also important for a sponsor to stay humble. By that I mean I have to share my stuff with my sponsees and stay open to learning from them and not be so arrogant that I feel I know it all and can tell them everything they need to do. Sometimes I'm in awe of the mystery that presents itself. Sometimes a sponsee presents a problem and I'll say, "I don't know; let's figure it out." I think those things help to cement that bond that allows the work to be done. If it's not there, the work won't get done.

ED: Work the steps in every area of your life. And when you don't, learn to laugh at yourself.

SOME SUGGESTIONS TO GIVE A NEWCOMER WHO HAS ASKED YOU TO SPONSOR HIM/HER.

M.T.: The suggestions given to me were simple—and numerous. In New York, where I got clean, at the beginning of almost every meeting, written into the format, were the suggestions (so every group acted as a collective sponsor to the newcomer): "If you're new, there are no rules in NA, but there are some suggestions." They went on to read: "Make ninety meetings in ninety days, and if that sounds like a lot make a meeting a day and the ninety will take care of itself [this made sense to me and told me I only had to worry about it a day at a time]; get a phone number at every meeting you go to so, at the end of ninety days, you will have ninety numbers; use the phone: a meeting is only an hour-and-a-half long; your disease is with you twenty-four hours a day. Get to meetings early and help set up, stay after and help clean up; sit up front, relax and listen, you may hear something that will help you to stay clean tonight; stay away from slippery people, places, and things—they will get you high before you get them clean." When I had 11 days, my sponsor asked me to write my first step.

LEIGH: They have to make at least ninety meetings in ninety days, to get phone numbers and to use them to call three people a day. They must make one or two meetings a day; some people need three meetings a day, depending on how they've used. What I recommend depends on the state they're in. If they're having seizures or not bathing, I tell them the most important thing is not to use. Some people have big problems going on, and I try to get them to focus on staying clean and the concept of having a successful day. If they're coherent, I'll have them write a first step.

J.P.: The first thing is to call me every day and leave a message if I'm not home. The main thing is that they go through the motions. If they want me to call back, they need to ask for it. I tell them to make meetings regularly. Sometimes there's a cloudy zone with people coming out of rehabs and detoxes who are exposed to multiple fellowships. I ask them to choose one fellowship. If they choose other than NA, I tell them they can call me until they find someone in the other fellowship. No one is left out in the cold.

NATALIE: I ask them, "To what lengths are you willing to go to for your sobriety? To what lengths are you willing to go to follow the program?" The "correct" response is, "Any lengths to change my life." If they're not sure, I tell them to ask themselves, "Why did I come in to AA?" When I first came in I wanted to do it my way. I thought you didn't understand that all my problems were everyone else's fault. Only later did I realize I was to blame. I was told to "just do it" and I did. That's how I pass it on.

JEANETTE: I tell them to keep a rock in their pocket to remind them to call their sponsor. I suppose calling every day is the most important thing. It begins to get them into good habits. I tell them to go to meetings, no set amount, because they won't be using in a meeting. If they're messed up, they need to be in a meeting. I feel my way along with the person I'm dealing with and then see what to suggest. Sometimes they just have to get comfortable going to meetings. I'll have them read the book so they become familiar with the program; it's not like a demand. Mostly, I get women with three, four, or five years clean, so I tell them just to read the *Twelve and Twelve* through.

KAREN: My suggestions to a newcomer: Make a meeting a day, especially if she is struggling on a daily basis to stay clean; if she isn't, I still suggest a meeting a day, but definitely not less than three or four times a week. I also suggest beginning prayer and meditation immediately and getting one number from each meeting and calling that person the next day just to get into the habit of doing so.

SUNNY: I tell a new sponsee to call me every day for the first month. Don't drink between meetings. Go to a meeting every day and read the AA sponsorship pamphlet so she has some sense of how this relationship works. I emphasize making meetings every day and that I'm there for her. I don't give her any other directions beyond these at first. But I do expect her to show up if she says she will.

PATRICE: I tell them AA is backwards; it's not how you feel, think, or believe that is important; it's taking recovery actions and to keep taking them until your feelings, thoughts, beliefs catch up with your actions. I tell them how this disease doesn't want them to recover, and it will try to stop them from being successful. It's going to tell them they're safe when their not, that they've done enough when they've barely started. The only way to beat this disease is to stay in action, stay connected with people in recovery. Recovery is really very simple; it's about learning how to spot danger, then acting appropriately. I go over the actions necessary to stay clean and sober (no set number of meetings, some may need several a day, others several a week). The most important thing is to get connected with recovering people and stay connected. This disease thrives on isolation. Most addicts and alcoholics are like the Lone Ranger who killed Tonto because they could do it better themselves.

SUZANNE: The first thing I suggest they do is create a schedule, just like a work schedule, of meetings they're going to go to on a regular basis and keep going back to. If they're just starting and don't know which ones they want to go to, I suggest very strongly that men go to all men's meetings (men's stag meetings) and women go to all women's meetings. I find the quality of sharing and authenticity is greater and the focus of sobriety, per se, is stronger in same gender meetings. I ask them to generate a schedule of where they're going to be every Monday, Tuesday, Wednesday, Thursday, Friday, Saturday, Sunday—what meetings they're going to be at, and work that out, so they commit to that and keep going back to those same meetings so people get to know them. I also suggest they start taking phone lists from the meetings they're going to and getting names and numbers from people and making a commitment: once a day they make a minimum of three program calls, to just call and say hello and check in with people from the meetings they go to, in order to start establishing phone relationships with people.

I have never been somebody who insisted somebody call me every day. I find most alcoholics don't take direction very well. If somebody is nearly sober, vacillating and wondering whether or not she is an alcoholic, that kind of expectation and direction may be overwhelming. So I may suggest that I'm available to her, and if she wants, she can call me. I also let her know that it probably would be helpful for her to check in with me, at least on my machine, on a daily basis, but I don't insist upon it.

CHARLES: I want them to call me every day; if I see they're going to meetings every day, I don't require that. But definitely, they have to call me once a week. They have to tell me what they've been doing. They have to meet with me regularly. I like to meet biweekly or every week for two hours at a time. And if they can't come to me, I go to them.

BOB: The calling every day becomes very inconvenient because you won't be able to get a hold of me every day. The constant home ringing and conferences on the phone . . . very often they're looking for a father, mother, friend, companion, or time-passer, rather than doing some step work. So, I really don't encourage it. In terms of periodic checking in, yes. Let me know what you're doing, how you are. There doesn't have to be a tragedy or anything. Just let me know how you're doing, once a week, once every couple of weeks, or whatever. It is a matter of constant, regular contact over a period of time, but no particular specified time period. You establish a time mode of when you feel like you need to be in touch with me. I feel that works more comfortably, as far as I'm concerned, than anything else.

They need to be writing the first three steps, before I even agree to sponsor them. That's just the first assignment: to write their feelings and their understanding of the first three steps.

MARIASHA: I ask that the woman call me, talk with me and get to know me. A lot of times, women in recovery houses are under pressure to get sponsors. Before I agree to sponsor somebody, I want to make sure there's a connection. I suggest they call me, and I will agree to be their interim sponsor until they make a decision whether or not it's working for them, so they don't feel under any obligation one way or another, but if they need to fulfill a commitment, they get that commitment fulfilled. I suggest they go to ninety meetings in ninety days when they're out of the recovery house, they get phone numbers of other women, and they listen, as opposed to sharing.

LISA: Don't pick up. Go to meetings. Reach out to newcomers. Share. I also tell them not to compare their recovery to anyone else's; I can only compare me to me.

BEA: I think they need to be in a meeting. Normally, I'll try to leave it open-ended; it's not like thirty or sixty. I know I needed to be in a meeting every night for the first year or more. So, I suggest they go to a meeting every night, to get three numbers of women at every meeting they go to, to sit up front, and to read.

I really think the sponsor/sponsee relationship is very special. I adore my sponsor. She has given me so much. I don't call her on a daily basis. Sometimes I don't call her on a weekly basis, but I stay in touch with her. She knows what's going on in my life, when there's a crisis or when there's a good time. It's just not as regular as when I was new. However, I'll have a new sponsee call me every day. I've sponsored several women: one woman with two years, one woman with three years, one woman going on five years; there's no need for them to call me every day, unless they're going through difficult periods. If they're going through a difficult period, and I see that it's a little dangerous

for them, I'll ask them, "I'd like you to call me every day."
But the truth is, I don't have time to talk on the phone to
four or five women every night and give them the feeling
that what they're telling me is important or the time to just
sit and listen and give feedback. But, at periods in their life,
when things are tough, and they're up against the wall, it's
fine. I'll always sponsor that newcomer right from the street.

DANNY: The basic direction I give them is to go to as
many meetings as possible. One of the things I've started
doing recently is giving them their first assignment: to share
at every meeting they attend. I've found it is very important
for them to participate in meetings. That's the basic one.
Another one is that they read the First Step and the *Basic
Text* over and over. If they see something that jumps out at
them, either underline it or highlight it, but just keep reading it, keep studying it, keep thinking about how it applies
to their lives, and not to use. Stay away from everything
that was a part of the pattern of using. Don't go back to the
places they used to go to. If they're in a relationship that
was something they used about, try to change the relationship or leave it alone for awhile. Basically, that's what I
suggest early on. I try to keep it simple: meetings, First
Step, share.

DON: My suggestions are make meetings and read the
Big Book and *Basic Text*, if you're literate. The essence of the
program is that we turn around our selfishness by helping
others, which also means to be of service, and then we get
happy. Those who aren't of service cheat themselves. They
don't catch on.

I modify my instructions all the time. Some only need
three meetings a week. It wouldn't hurt if they went to
more meetings, but if they were only a minimal drug user,
they don't need seventeen meetings a week. I let them de-

....

cide until the first slip they have—after that they must follow my directions. But I don't believe in blanket recovery.
I look at what they are doing in their lives. Do they have a
full-time job? Five kids? Mortgage payments? Work 12 A.M.
to 8 A.M.? If they've got major attachments, I feel it's unreasonable to ask them to make a meeting a day. They say
make ninety meetings in ninety days. I think if you're going
to make a meeting a day it should be for a year. Where did
ninety come from? It's arbitrary. The ninety days is considered the amount of time to engage people in the program.
If a sponsee has nothing else to do, he should make meetings
every day. Everything else is semi-important compared to
saving their lives. I modify my demands on my babies (sponsees). Ninety and ninety always sounds like a demand, not
a suggestion. I want to keep their level of frustration down.

MARGE: Just a couple of basic ones; one is to go to a
step study meeting (where they read the step and then discuss it) at least once a week. Another one is to start reading
the book *Alcoholics Anonymous*. Another one would be to have
a discussion about where they are with a Higher Power in
their lives and some suggestions as to what they could do
to start working on their relationship with God. I think
that's what it's all about. If they wait until the Eleventh Step
to really get into that, the quality of their previous steps is
going to suffer immensely, and they're going to miss the
spiritual awakenings because they haven't placed themselves
in the process. And the magic, if you want to call it that, is
in the spiritual experiences and awakenings. People who
don't dive into that never seem to be happy they're sober.
It's like jumping in a pool instead of just putting your foot
in water and taking it out. My mentor Tris used to call it
"jumping off the lighted plynth"—going from this safe spot
into the darkness, but having the faith to do so—that's the

surrender. If you miss that, you miss the spiritual and are literally fighting off alcohol one day at a time, which is not what I think our program's about.

ED: First, when they ask how it works, there's the old tried and true: "Don't pick up, go to meetings, and change your whole life." That always seems to relax them, to make them smile. Then, I usually tell them how I got clean:

- Don't pick up. (If you don't pick up, you won't get loaded.)

- Go to meetings, a meeting a day for the first ninety days.

- Get hold of the *Basic Text* and read it from cover to cover.

- Relax. Don't worry about sharing, just sit back and listen.

- When you do share, share from your heart. (Don't try to impress us with how intelligent you are; we know you're a jerk.)

- Take it easy. You don't have to know how it works, none of us do. Just keep showing up and one of these days it'll get you.

- Remember, you're in the right place.

    My favorite one is:

- You're okay just the way you are. You just don't know it.

LOIS: If they're new to the program, I ask them to look up the operative words in Step One, to write about how they are powerless over their addiction, and to write about what it means to have an unmanageable life. I give them my phone numbers and ask them to call me once a day for thirty days, and also to call whenever they need to.

If they've been around a while, I discuss their understanding of the step and how powerlessness applies in many, many areas of their lives. I give them any of the above assignments if it seems needed, and I suggest we meet and discuss what they want to accomplish at this stage of their program and to tell me something of their background. I ask them to call me regularly for thirty days. The purpose of the thirty-day calling is so they memorize your phone number and get into the regular habit of calling you.

THE MOST IMPORTANT THINGS TOLD TO OUR SPONSORS BY THEIR SPONSORS.

SUZANNE: There are many things. One of them is time, about moving into the future and dealing with changes. When I didn't know how to do something, she's always said, "You don't have to know how. God knows how." When I was newly sober, things were a big deal for me. She did something with me that was very helpful: she'd say, "Okay, I'm going to write this down right now, and I'm going to ask you about it later." And two weeks, even a month, later she'd say, "Remember what was going on February twelfth, at 12:00 in the afternoon, that was such a big deal?" I could never remember it. It helped me put into perspective that all of this fear-driven, negative drama I would generate really wasn't a big deal, except in my own mind. It helped me become more grounded and get a better perspective on life.

CHARLES: He told me I was not the program. He also said I was not the message either. I remember that most of all. And the best thing I could do was to drive over and pick somebody up and take them to a meeting.

LEIGH: Feelings aren't facts. Working with others. To read. To keep working my program. That I could call at any time. I needed to know I could call.

M.T.: That you can go through recovery as many people do—dragging your feet—or you can soar like a bird. The best is to soar. That's the real reason we're in recovery, for the spiritual awakening. All of us in these fellowships have one thing in common—the fact that we feel disconnected from society in a profound way. The steps, the spiritual awakening, get us connected in a profound way.

BEA: Things that build my self-discipline, like having me sit in the front of the room, just sit. When I'm at a meeting, as a newcomer, in the first few years, to sit in the front of the room and just listen. My sponsor taught me so many things; she taught me about compulsiveness and that the opposite of compulsiveness is control, thinking things out. She taught me a lot about spirit, about God. I had big trouble with God; it was a big problem. She had me doing spiritual affirmations, and she made me commit to doing them for short periods of time. I always did them. I had so much ego that, if I said I was going to do them, I did them. With me, even if I didn't want to do it, I had so much ego, I just got up and did it anyway, grudgingly, but I did it. That's the stuff that changed me. And I guess that comes back to discipline too, self-discipline. When I call my sponsor, when something's going on, she makes my actions real clear for me. I feel like she knows me well. She'll put the step out that applies; she goes right to whichever it is, just pulls it and makes it clear for me. That's what I can give to the women that I sponsor. That's what I try to give. I don't know if I do, but I try to.

DANNY: One of the most important things I heard was that I had to get rid of my reservations about using, that I had to make a total surrender. I was around here for a long time (five or six years) before I did that. It was the fact that I had to do it for myself. I think those are the two strongest, most important things I got, aside from the basics that everybody hears in meetings and reads in the *Basic Text*. It's really losing your reservations and not trying to do it for somebody else or to please somebody else. One more thing is that I'm not a bad person. I had to be told that a whole lot, because I came in with a lot of guilt, and that was the cycle that kept me using. The fact that this is a new life is such a message.

DON: My sponsor taught me about love. About getting involved in service. We've talked and done inventories ever since. He taught me it was about cleaning up our stuff and changing the way we've been. God has created a miracle, so, "Don't mess up the miracle." He helped me to discern what's valid from invalid. He gave me direction other than "share with the group" when someone's not around to share with. I tell my sponsees, "Your hand doesn't need to be up at every meeting unless you have a problem." Now I know how to work a program.

MARGE: The first thing is God is the answer to just staying physically sober, not that God's not the answer to everything, but once I released any control of the drinking or using and allowed that to reside with my Higher Power, I had a marvelous freedom to work the rest of the steps and start unloading what was in the way of loving for me. Without that first process, I would've expended a lot of energy fighting off alcohol and staying sober; I don't think that's necessary at all. I had a lot of emotional work to do, and I simply could not have gone through those processes, or today go through those processes on different levels, while fighting off alcohol and drugs with my other hand. This doesn't work that way.

The other thing I was told that made this absolutely the highest calling in my life at this time was that I can be involved. I always thought I had a purpose, but I had no clue what that was. There were some things that were told to me that made staying sober, and helping other alcoholics to achieve sobriety was absolutely the most marvelous thing I was meant to do. I was told the drinking part of alcoholism was neither bad or good, it was a state of being other than recovery, and the whole point was to move into recovery. But I hear a lot of people in AA justifying being in the recovery experience by having to constantly reaffirm that their drinking experience was bad. If it was that bad, we would not have done it. Alcoholics are a lot of things, but we are not stupid. If it wasn't working for us or if we had an indication that it was all over, most of us got sober, but, as long as there was a glimmer of hope, we kept using that remedy, that solution.

Recovery is a state of being; sobriety is a state of being; it's ongoing and not static—it's ever unfolding. To become immersed in the program from the very beginning, it's the most important thing I can do. Tris talked about the difference between having a map (which is having the steps in writing) and being in the territory (which means incorporating those steps internally and immersing yourself in that process, instead of standing outside of the process) as being the most important thing you can do. I believe that was true for me. I see it being true for the people I sponsor. The preciousness of the ability to love, which comes out of discarding whatever is in the way of that, has been stressed to me over and over and over again. I think it's because I didn't know that's what I was looking for when I came here. I was looking for loving and the ability to love and had no idea that's what I was seeking. That has been made clear to me through sponsors over and over and over again, either verbally or by loving me or providing me with a nonjudgemental pool in which to do my work. I've realized that's what I'm here for. Tris used to say that alcoholism is actually the cure for what is reporting to be the disease.

MARIASHA: The most healing thing my sponsor has ever said to me is there aren't any rules, except that you can't use and be in my house. Whenever I've called her with any kind of self-reproach for not doing what I should be doing, or could be doing, or not meeting any expectations with her, whether they be mine or hers, she has always comforted me and said, "I don't have any expectations of you; I'm here to support you; you call me as often as you need to, or you feel you want to. But, I don't need anything more from you than for you to utilize me at whatever pace you feel comfortable." I think that's been the most important thing for me and what I pass on, that being sponsored should not be a pressure. She has never put any kind of pressure or burden on me.

J.P.: The power of prayer: through it, all things are attainable. To do it from the heart. That the answer to the disease is the program. The answer to the program is the steps. The answer to the steps is God.

ED: To keep it simple. When I finished with my step work, I asked him what to do next. He said, "Now you live your life." That's it. No search for the Holy Grail, no pie in the sky intellectual theory, just a simple showing up for life.

He's not one for intellectual musing. He goes more for the heart. And I've noticed he's right. When someone is sharing from his head, it may be fun for a while, but then it gets meaningless. When someone shares from his heart, he has my complete attention. Somehow you can tell. I don't know how, but you can. So I try to stay out of my head.

He says a sponsor is someone who helps you to sort out your head, because he has some distance from you. You are too close to what's going on in your head.

I had a really complicated, intellectual way of working the steps with my sponsees. When I showed it to him, after he finished laughing, he suggested I simplify it. I did.

PATRICE: There were several things she said to me that I feel were very important to my recovery. One of them was her ability to sound like a broken record each time we talked, stressing to me not to drink or use, no matter what! I think she said it that often so that each and every one of my cells got the message. She did that throughout my first year and well into my second, after that only on special occasions such as disasters or celebrations. She also brought my attention to my abusive "self-talk." She even hung up the phone on me one day, saying she never listens to anyone bad mouth a friend of hers the way I was bad mouthing myself! She told me to think of someone I loved and ask myself what would I say to this person if this had happened in his or her life, then to say this to myself. She really helped me to learn to be more accepting and more loving of myself.

One other thing she said was that if I did what others had done before me, my insides would match my outside. That was pretty important to me because I never matched. I always walked around feeling like if you really knew me you wouldn't like me. I didn't show that, nor did I show how frightened, lonely, and shy I was around people.

....

JEANETTE: One of the most important things my sponsor told me was that my problems were not out there, they were internal. I always complained about my husband, life, etc. She made me focus on what was wrong with me, not society, the medical profession, the school system, etc.

BOB B.: I guess the biggest thing my sponsor Sandy told me is I could tell him anything. I could be honest, regardless of what it was. I wouldn't be put down, and I would be treated as a friend, rather than him reacting as more an adviser or some doctor. He was just another person. Let's talk on that level, talking the gut level down.

Chapter Two

Gender Issues

"*I don't have any problem with men sponsoring women. The bigger thing is the reasons for doing it.*"

— BOB B.

Should you agree to sponsor someone of the opposite sex? Some thoughts on gay sponsorship: Is same sex/sexual preference sponsorship a problem? Are there special considerations when taking on a sponsee who is HIV+?

It is generally accepted that you choose someone of the same sex as your sponsor to "keep it simple" and avoid unnecessary sex-related problems from arising. Also, the idea is to share with someone that you can relate to, because they too are male or female. Like a good big brother or sister—you're in the same family but they're older and have more experience. But what about people in recovery who are gay or lesbian? If they choose the same sex, they are also choosing sexual preference. If they choose the opposite sex, are they confronted with forming an intimate relationship with someone they may not be able to relate to because they may have less in common? What if you're heterosexual and you are asked by someone of the opposite sex to be their sponsor? What do you say? In the first part of the chapter, our sponsors address these questions.

The second part of this chapter deals with HIV+ people in recovery and some of the experiences of people who have sponsored them. This section will be enlightening to those in recovery who have been reluctant to sponsor people with HIV+ conditions, those who are sponsoring them, and those who have the disease.

SHOULD YOU AGREE TO SPONSOR
SOMEONE OF THE OPPOSITE SEX?

BOB B.: I don't have any problem with men sponsoring women. The bigger thing is the reasons for doing it. I think we have to know what our motives are to process them, and not have any problems with being willing to change the situation if problems arise. It might be okay at the moment, but it might be wrong tomorrow. Right now, I'm not really confronted with that particular issue, but I'm not really against it. I think sometimes it could be a plus because sometimes we communicate different things to the opposite sex and sometimes there might be individuals who need that type of communication. Hopefully, the person he chooses to communicate with is going to direct him in a certain way, can get the information he needs, or be sensitive to his well being, and directly guide him through what the steps are and not just a lot of personal things that become involved which are not directly related to recovery.

MARIASHA: This is one of those unwritten NA rules that irritates me. I was asked only once by a gay man if I would sponsor him. It was a step study meeting in Hollywood that I attended regularly. It was mostly men who attended this meeting, but there were a few women. He felt he always identified with what I shared, that I had wisdom, and he wanted to reap the benefits of that wisdom. Would I work with him? It was a real struggle for me; I don't like to say no to somebody who is in need of help and is willing. But NA has this unspoken position: men work with men and women work with women. I suggested he could call me, and I'd be happy to talk with him. But I encouraged him to try to make a connection with another male, to look for the similarities rather than the differences. I tried to talk to him about what his resistance was about,

....

in terms of not wanting to work with a man, to help him look at the competitiveness and the jealousy. I also tried to show him he was setting himself apart instead of seeing similarities, which was preventing him from finding a man that he could work with. I availed myself to him by phone. But he really didn't take too much advantage of it. He's called periodically through the years, when he has something that he's struggling with. I have mixed feelings about this. I don't work with people of the opposite sex. I'm not a man; I don't have the experiences of men. I think feelings cross socioeconomic status, racial status, and man/woman stuff. I don't know if you have to have had the same experience in order to be helpful to another human being. When I lost a baby and I was grieving, the people I got the most support from were people who were tender and sensitive. They weren't people who necessarily lost babies. All that did was affirm that you don't have to have the identical reality to benefit. So, could I help a man, not being a man? Probably, because people are people and feelings cross all those different lines. I think there's a part of me that's a people-pleaser. I don't choose to stir a lot of controversy.

MARGE: I've sponsored several men. I've found that men don't ask me to sponsor them unless it's really meant to be. We're either very, very similar, or both the women and the men who I've sponsored usually have some issues dealing with sex they need to talk about and have the freedom to talk about. That's an area where I'm pretty okay. I asked my sponsor about that once, and she, with thirty-two years, said the case in which a woman can be helpful to a man is simply where someone is sexually unsure or has sexual questions and needs someone to be honest with him. Men tend to be able to talk to women more than they do men about such things. I've found that in my own experience. Usually the men have moved on and gotten a male sponsor after I've done whatever work that seemed to be right with them. I think in the flip side of that, I've benefited totally from Tris, but he was not my sponsor. I think whether a woman gets a male sponsor depends absolutely on whether she has been used to manipulating men. The reason I think we have that line in AA is because we are ill-fitted to determine that when we're first sober. We simply repeat the same behavior sober that we did drinking, except it has a nicer facade on it. So, in order to prevent that kind of stuff, I think that's why we have the rule. But, I think everyone is different, and I don't have any problems with whatever the hookup is if it benefits both people.

BEA: I'd love to but I can't. I just couldn't. I've thought about it. I had a guy ask me if I'd be his sponsor. We just have such different needs. I really believe the men should be with the men and the women with the women. If I were to have had a male sponsor, my recovery would've been much different, I'm sure.

M.T.: One of the cutest guys ever to walk into the rooms asked me to sponsor him. He was twenty-six (a few years younger than me), tall, and would have shown his good looks to his best advantage if he wasn't such a mess. He was in NA on a court order that expired after thirty meetings. He seemed interested in the program, asked questions, went to coffee with the group and read the *Basic Text*. All of these things were more than the court required, so it seemed the program was taking hold. When he asked me to sponsor him, I said no at first and told him to find a male sponsor. I could see the potential for problems. He said he'd been around for twenty days or so at that time, and though he liked the program, he hadn't heard any guys speak that

....

he felt in the least inspired by or was willing to take direction from. But, he had felt very encouraged by the things he'd heard me share and thought I could help him stay clean. He said if I didn't feel comfortable sponsoring him, that was fine, but he wasn't going to stick around otherwise—his court requirement was almost up. He thought if he started working the steps he might be more compelled to stay, but otherwise he was gone. I should have said toot-a-loo, but I felt this was a person who was willing to work a program and who I could help, and it just happened he was male. Also, he was so messed up—abnormally thin, barely able to put sentences together, the fog was so thick in his brain. He wasn't at all physically appealing. So I figured if it doesn't work out, I can easily tell him to go to someone else. What a mistake! Things were okay for the first couple of months and then, through a combination of events (I was lonely after a guy who'd made promises let me down, etc.), this sponsee and I ended up having an affair that lasted eighteen months! People in New York, my first friends and advisors in NA, said when a person with time gets involved with a newcomer, it's the person with time who suffers—not the newcomer! It's the truth. I almost went out over doing so. I knew better, and I should not have let my screwed up thinking make the decision. I felt so ashamed in recovery that I felt I had no place to go—that is one of the worst feelings I've ever had. The pain was intense. In theory, I don't have a problem with the idea of cross-sex sponsorship, and I'm sure in practice some people are finding success with it, but if I were ever going to attempt it again, I would analyze every angle, and look high and low at the damage potential. I think as Bob B. says, the important thing is the reason you're doing it. I did it for the right reasons, but at the point it was getting beyond the recovery arena, when I should have cut it loose, it was already too late.

DANNY: Aside from the fact that it's suggested that we don't do it, I can see any number of situations where I wouldn't know what to do, would not have a clue. The reason we sponsor the same sex is because we tend to have some similar life experiences from a point of view that makes it work. I have some relationships with women in the program where sometimes I almost feel like a sponsor. We have such a rapport; we talk a lot about what's going on with each other. Just the other day I talked to woman who's got nine months. She has a relationship with a sponsor, but we have a rapport as well, and there are some things that we relate to because we're close to the same age, some background similarities. She'll tell me what's going on, and it may be similar to what's been going on with me. So we get into some stuff. In fact, I gave her some direction. It's not like, "I want you to do this." It's more like, "You ought to think about this." I would never think I could sponsor a woman, but I can certainly be her friend and offer things to her in the program. On an official basis, it's just too weird. Also, if I decide to have a gathering of my sponsees and here's this one woman, the guys are not going to loosen up. Or the other way, with a room full of women and one guy.

J.P.: My ex-wife sponsored husbands and their wives and that was a very, very poor decision. When things were not good between the couple, the discussion on issues became a search for information on the other person.

No, either way—men sponsoring women and women sponsoring men. I've seen it happen that men who are sponsored by women are looking for affection (mothering usually), and it has nothing to do with recovery. I think it's belligerent and shows contempt for the program if you're a man sponsoring women and women with men unless you're gay.

PATRICE: I've sponsored men, but only for a temporary time until we found them male sponsors. I've also worked as a step sponsor for a man who came to me for help for one or two steps such as Six, Seven and Eight.

NATALIE: Sometimes it's okay for women to have male sponsors when they can't relate to women. My experience was that women were jealous of me so I fixed on men.

SUZANNE: I think it's preferable (for men to be with men and women with women) because I think it keeps boundaries clean and relationships don't inadvertently become sexualized. However, if someone is mature enough, and clear enough, I think she can be very helpful to someone of the opposite gender. It's good as an interim sponsor relationship, because sometimes a girl has been abused by her mother, so she doesn't trust women in the beginning and would never be able to get guidance from a woman, or get a sponsor who was a woman, in the beginning of her recovery. So, the best she can do is to be in a relationship with a man, until she gets to that place where that healing has occurred. And vice versa, men to women.

IS SAME SEX/SEXUAL PREFERENCE SPONSORSHIP A PROBLEM?

CHARLES: I've sponsored both straight and gay people. I think what comes up for me as a *gay* person is not to be *prejudiced* against people who are gay and to own that homophobia. As far as AA and gay and all that, I think the biggest thing that's wrong with all of us is we get into our own little ghettos. We have our own group; we have our own best friend; we have our sponsor, and that's it. That's not it. You have to have those three things, yes. But what you need to do is also be willing to reach out, just like the book says, and to bring other things in. If we forget to bring in those other things we need, that have to do with our sexuality or anything else, we deprive ourselves, we become an island. I think that's one of the states we could fall into: we create our own little ghetto. My advice is this: I don't want to live in a ghetto, and I don't want my sponsees to live in one.

I think that I have the ability to work with anybody. As far as someone being able to pull anything over me, that is total crap. Anyway, why are we here? Is it to pull something over on each other? If we're not honest with our sponsor and don't tell him everything that's going on, than why are we being sponsored?

LEIGH: I am lesbian, and my first sponsor was a gay man, and I felt safe with him. It was a deep relationship. Again, sponsorship is a primary, nonsexual relationship. Today, I have a heterosexual woman as my sponsor. I've had straight men, gay men, gay women. I have sponsored straight and gay men and women. The most successful relationships are with straight men. There was never a sexual issue. I think the boundaries between intimacy and sexuality can get very thin. Straight men learned to develop a friendship with me that couldn't be sexual. You transcend a lot of boundaries as a sponsor. I sponsored a straight woman in Amsterdam who was sicker than others. She said, "I want to sleep with you." I told her, "That is not what sponsorship is about, and I don't want to sleep with you." She was a knockout, but that wasn't the issue. I had a lesbian who asked me over to hear her First Step. She made me dinner and wanted to read me her first step by candlelight. I said, "What is going on here?" I turned the lights on and said, "Let's do this at the table, not in your bedroom." She said, "I fancy you." I was really thrown. I told her, "I've been dealing with you as a sponsee.'' I was attracted to her, and she was gay. But I thought, ''No can do.'' If sexuality is an issue and you're willing to deal with it and you're in gay NA, then get a male sponsor. If you're a woman, vice versa. Some gay women will only trust gay women. It depends on where you are in your evolution. I need to have a woman sponsor because there are issues that men don't understand. Then again, nothing's straight with me in it. You can co-sponsor, work together if you don't have a choice.

DON: There was a straight newcomer guy who tried to catch women at the straight meetings he was attending. He couldn't resist, and he couldn't stay clean either. I suggested he only make gay meetings, which he did and that worked. He could focus on the recovery without temptations. In straight AA, it's men with men and women with women, which I agree with. If not, it can spoil relationships later. We (gays) are no different. If you're gay/lesbian and really want to focus on your program, have someone of the op-posite sex sponsor you. It keeps everything on a nonsexual basis. I've run into it as a problem. I've done some sleazy things in sobriety. I say to someone who is gay, get a woman sponsor but interact with men and women. Men can go to a men's stag if there's an issue they can't talk about with their female sponsors. I always thought it was a good idea for lesbians to get someone of the opposite sex. If you're gay, I would admonish to make sure you don't dilute the program, don't alter it or change it just because you're gay and think some things don't apply. The program works equally for straight and gay. God is a miracle for the person not for the sexual preference.

MARGE: A gay woman wandered in to 26th and Broad-way [a meeting place in California] one afternoon, and the older men were sitting around paying attention to her. This woman was shaking badly. I took her in the back room and got her some coffee and talked to her. She had been in the gay AA community for a long time, had been lying to them and taking [anniversary] cakes when she wasn't sober and participating in the social life there on levels that were not conducive to her well being. I was very frank with her. I had observed that emotionally, gay meetings were not always a good place for somebody who was new, who needed to work the steps. So, I offered to sponsor her if she would go to regular AA meetings and work her steps. She agreed. I didn't find any problem with that. I think dysfunction is dysfunction, whether you're green, purple, or brown, whether you're gay or straight. The drama that goes with dysfunctional gay relationships is the same drama that goes with dysfunctional heterosexual relationships. So all of the things that don't serve you if you're straight, don't serve you if you're gay. Love is love. It's the same process.

ARE THERE SPECIAL CONSIDERATIONS WHEN TAKING ON A SPONSEE WHO IS HIV+?

CHARLES: If people who are HIV+ should only have HIV+ sponsors, I'd be limiting myself with the amount of people I sponsor. I do think they should go to an HIV+ meeting once a week. Yes, I think that is definitely important if they're HIV+. Or they should be active in the community by teaching about HIV. Or they should have some program where they're involved, where that helps them with that issue. I also think it's good if you're going to sponsor HIV+ people, that you should have some training, that you should go and seek out information, outside of what you learn in the *Big Book*. I think it's impossible to speak on anything unless you have some experience in it. I'm not experienced personally with being HIV+, but I am getting experience from the community. I'm learning with my friends that are HIV+, and I do attend an HIV+ meeting once a month.

What consideration should you make in taking on HIV+ sponsees? Are you willing to go the full distance with these people? Are you willing to give all? I think willingness is everything—willingness to learn about things you don't know about. Turning down a sponsee because he is HIV+ wouldn't be something I would do. But I'm not speaking for what other people should do. I feel the consideration I should have is, "Am I willing to see them get well, or am I willing to see them go through whatever they have to go through?"

One thing that comes up with people who are HIV+ is, Do they have support there? I cannot be there for total support for that issue. Therefore, they have to be in some other support group. As long as they'll go out and be supported in the community by other things, and to help them in that area, they can also be a support for me, too, in helping me understand it. I see it as a bridge.

ED: There are no considerations. Anyone can sponsor anyone. Which is more important? The problem or the solution? We are all human. We are all going to die. Sometimes it seems that HIV+ people act as though they're the only people on earth who will die. All we really have is this moment. That's it. We talk about having one foot in the past and one foot in the future and pissing on today. The steps teach us to live in this moment. Life is a gift. Everything we have is on loan to us.

People with HIV tend to think their impending death is more important than this moment. I try to bring their attention back to this moment. I suggest they learn how to meditate. I tell them to read Suzuki's *Zen Mind, Beginner's*

Mind. I listen to their problems and then ask them what they can do about it. Can they do anything? If not, can they accept that this is the way things are?

BEA: I really think it's good if you're HIV+ to find an HIV+ sponsor. But sometimes it just doesn't seem like there are enough people with time. There are a couple of women that I've sponsored who have had the virus. What I try to bring to them is that their disease of addiction will kill them before their disease of AIDS, and they need to focus on that because it's really easy not to.

There are very definite, special considerations. One of the women I sponsored seemed unable, a lot of the time, to do things when it came to her recovery work. But, it was really hard for me to call her on that stuff, because I just didn't know how to react. I found a lot of times she wasn't able to do the step work, or she just had no energy, or I thought she just wasn't willing. I would just try to remind her that her disease of addiction was going to kill her more quickly than her disease of AIDS. I also tell her to remember that addiction is her primary disease. For a while there she couldn't write, and using a tape recorder, she started the steps, which was great. That is the point: you have to get out of your head, out in the universe, on the paper, in the air. There were a couple of women who I sponsored where I made sure that we went to HIV+ meetings. I had them meet other women who were dealing with the same problems, because there are so many more problems to being HIV+. So it's hard, really hard. You need to have a lot of patience and a lot of love to give. Before taking on another woman who is HIV+, I think I'd probably like to have fewer sponsees, just to be able to devote my time to her.

DON: Sponsoring people with AIDS made me a better person. It put my program to the test. I had to ask myself,

"Am I going to be of service, no matter what? Will I love them if they have Carposi on their face and can't hold their bowels? Am I going to be there for someone when he takes his last breath?" The answer is yes.

The important things are to listen and be able to make correct referrals for hospitalization, memorial services, etc. They have to face their death, talk about it. And you have to walk very carefully through this. Some people with AIDS get angry if you mention it. They're in denial. They think you're being negative. They say, "No. I'm going to live; I'm going to beat it." You have to wait until the day they ask you about your thoughts on heaven and dying, when they're not scared to talk about it.

I would trust most people in the fellowship with sponsoring people with AIDS. You do things you wouldn't with others, like picking up groceries. When they find out they're HIV+, let them talk about it or go home and go to bed and cover their heads. Tell them it's okay to do that.

One sponsee thought I would throw him away when he told me he was HIV+. I told him I suffer from a disease deadlier than AIDS. Alcoholism is more deadly. AIDS takes longer to kill people, and it's a better death than alcoholism.

It's been my experience that people with AIDS want to work the steps. The most beautiful thing in the world is to watch someone with AIDS start to work the steps. They get dignity in their lives, and when they die, they do it with dignity. I've seen people die both ways, and it's not pretty either way. But with a program in their lives, they're not as scared, and they have more dignity. It's brought tears to my eyes to watch that.

If they have AIDS, they are going to have to take medication. Some of them are addicting. You must ask them, when they reach for the bottle, to think, Is this the appropriate time to take these drugs? The body can't tell the difference. Be aware. Keep the drugs under scrutiny. Make sure they know what they're taking. Doctors give Marinol for lack of appetite. It's a marijuana derivative that helps them eat. Some AIDS patients take tranquilizers like Valium to sleep. They take a lot of different drugs.

They're not to be sacrificial martyrs, but they should be full of knowledge and sponsor's knowledge. I make sure to throw away sponsees' drugs when they've died. Lovers often slip on others' drugs. You can donate leftover AZT and Bactrim to AIDS victims in Mexico.

DANNY: I've had the experience of knowing someone in the fellowship who was HIV+. I've got a very dear friend that's HIV+, who goes through things with his HIV+ sponsees. When a person with AIDS asked me to sponsor him, he was very open about it. He was just very matter of fact about it. I guess because he was so open, and the way he looked at me, I just said, "Yeah." The first thing that came to mind was, I need to know more about this. I get phone feedback and updates on his health. I try to stay in touch with him as much as possible, ask him how he was doing and what was going on. Some things he told me about I understood, others I didn't. There are a lot of terms and words that I don't know yet. But, there are some logical things I know he should be doing or shouldn't be doing. We talked about those things. I know he has a good foundation in his other disease. Regardless of how a person acquired the disease, I think it takes a special person to sponsor somebody who is HIV+. Because, someplace down the line, you're going to have various things that happen. You can't be afraid to hug him, talk about it, go visit him, or whatever. You have to be there anyway, and, if you're not strong enough to do that, you have to pass. Unfortunately, there's a lot of fear in the fellowship, but there's also a lot of love. I think, in terms of his recovery, I feel real confident about sponsoring him within that realm. In terms of his additional illness, I told him some of that he has to do himself with HIV+ meetings and possibly some support groups that the community organizations sponsor.

BOB B.: I have had to look at their medical problems. I'm not a doctor; I can't be specific about what kind of medication they should or shouldn't take. I think they should be open, in terms of not hiding what's going on. Once again, we have to get out of that hiding place. So, the only negative thing I find is it becomes about survival; it has a lot to do with quality of living and sometimes just a case of walking the journey with him. Because, as with any other type of the illness of that nature, I think everyone wants to feel like they're not alone. They don't want to feel like they're a cancer to all the associates they're with. So, they really need a friend. I think that's one of the main things, trying to be a friend and know that they're trying to take care of themselves the best they can, that they're trying different avenues of where like groups of people associate and congregate. Sometimes it becomes a question of them feeling sorry for themselves, those things come into play and then they need guidance. I'll just help the person make it from day to day. There are others around. They do have support groups, and we try to direct them to the support groups for that part of it.

It is important for them to have a person who is empathic, caring, and understanding as to the nature of the disease and to act as a guide or example to the person that is sponsored and, in addition, to the world at large. I think it's a case of feeling good about himself and what's going on, about living and the pursuits of living, the quality of living, and those types of things. They have some eye on that, looking forward, looking upward. Not doing better.

SUZANNE: I don't think it's any different than any other sponsor/sponsee relationship, except for the fact that for those who are HIV+ there's much more of an urgency to go deeper into the spiritual aspects of the program. So, you can't take the same amount of time to go through things. You'd have to do it more rapidly, because of the urgency of their lives. To connect with themselves in a deep spiritual way, and with others, is much more present.

Chapter Three

Sponsor/Sponsee Relationships

"I was told that a sponsor/sponsee relationship is a friendship formed for the mutual benefit of both."

—JEANETTE

Is it necessary or important to develop a
friendship (i.e., socialize) with your sponsee or
just be there to give direction with the steps
and working the program? What is fair for the
sponsor to expect from the sponsee?

*Being a sponsor means sharing your experience, strength and
hope and taking a personal interest in another person's recovery, walking your sponsee through the steps and through
the ups and downs in their recovery. Does that automatically
mean you need to be friends as well? If you've been wondering
exactly what type of relationship you should have with your
sponsee/sponsor, a friendship or only a mentorship, you will
find some interesting answers here.*

*When people come to you for help, to be their sponsor,
they have certain expectations of you and what you will share
with them. But what can, or should, sponsors expect from
their sponsees?*

IS IT NECESSARY OR IMPORTANT TO DEVELOP A FRIENDSHIP OR TO SOCIALIZE WITH YOUR SPONSEE? IS IT OKAY TO JUST BE THERE TO GIVE DIRECTION WITH THE STEPS AND WORKING THE PROGRAM?

J.P.: I've found that if I become friendly with my sponsees, they call less. I don't like to be their friend because
we wind up in too much small talk. I don't want to gab
about baseball, football, or the weather and lose track of the

life issues. It's important we talk about the things that are going on in their recovery. I don't have the time to waste. Even if I only gave them five minutes each, that's an hour a day! It's a lot. Out of twelve, I only have one sponsee that I socialize with.

M.T.: This is a tough question. On the one hand, I think you need to know a person well to sponsor her—how she thinks, what's going on in her daily life, etc.—in order to be able to direct her on working Steps Six, Seven, Eight, Nine, and Ten on a regular basis. Being in very regular contact, sharing her troubled times as well as her accomplishments, seeing her through situations, seeing her progress, is what it's about. So, in some ways a friendship evolves naturally as I bond with my sponsee. But friends are chosen by both parties, where as in recovery, as a rule sponsees choose sponsors. The criteria for friends are much different than those of sponsor/sponsee, although the dynamic is similar in some ways. The sponsor and sponsee relationship is based on inequality—one person has more experience, knowledge, and wisdom than the other; one is "older," as measured by time in the fellowship. I don't think I can't like my sponsees, but I'm not sure how important that is either, as long as they're doing the work. Also, a friendship tends to equalize the participants, and I do believe it's important that the sponsor retain the "upper hand"—being in a position of more of a mentor than a friend. It should remain clear as the relationship progress that the sponsor is there to give direction and the sponsee is supposed to be willing to follow it. Naturally, as time goes on, sponsees learn about their sponsor's human frailties, but keeping your sponsor in a special place is good. I think it's good to look up to someone and hear her words above everyone else's—if you trust her and respect her recovery (which should be the standard you had to begin with when you chose her). I think sponsees should find buddies in the fellowship and rely on their sponsor for guidance with the steps and with important decisions in their lives, decisions that affect their recovery and their program. These days, I feel like I don't want to be friends with my sponsees, to socialize with them to any degree. I have friends I love that I hardly get to see as it is! So to take on someone who is asking for my guidance with their program and then to add more than I'm probably able to fulfill, I believe, is unwarranted and unnecessary.

BOB B.: Yes, we try to do some social things together; hopefully we try to become "friends," because that's how you become more intimate in terms of knowing something about the person. I found, when possible, it's a good rule of thumb to have some intimate exchanges, whether it's going to dinner or a show, or going out with some other people picnicking, whatever the case may be. Doing some personal, private things is really where you get to see the true person, more so than you can in settings where you don't get a chance to really know what your person's about. It is important to see him act in a natural sense rather than a fixed, pretentious sense. His fronts are let down. You get a chance to see behind the facade of who he thinks he is. It becomes very necessary and very important in terms of getting a chance to know that person. You'll be able to respond to that person a lot more in a different, more informed way.

You get a friendship going and very often you find it helps you in terms of working with the person. The more involved you become, though not getting overinvolved, the better in terms of making life decisions. It's just a good relationship to get to know the person. I think more is achieved in that type of relationship than we can realize by just going to meetings. You really don't get to know the person. There's much to be learned about our personalities in relationships with one another, in terms of a long term, interactive one, or a different level than just going to a meeting and meeting on a casual basis.

SUNNY: I sponsor some people I don't care for too much. I'm there to answer their questions and see them at meetings. I have one sponsee who is depressed and hardly uses me anymore—she got angry with me. One separated and came back and is now closer than ever. I've been fired a few times, which hurt my feelings. One said, "I don't need another mother."

KAREN: The relationship I have with sponsees, once we've worked the steps, is that of good friend. I'm always there for them, even if we haven't talked in a long time, just like my sponsor is there for me. We talk occasionally just to stay current, and I call her whenever something specific comes up.

I try to cultivate a trusting relationship prior to step work. I like to meet a few times in and out of meetings to just talk about the circumstances of their life, their using, what brought them here, etc. I share my story as well. I like for us to know each other and trust each other (have a friendship) before delving into the more intense steps.

JEANETTE: I was told that a sponsor/sponsee relationship is a friendship formed for the mutual benefit of both.

PATRICE: I have worked with women that I had nothing in common with in the beginning except we were both recovering. Friendship, or rather a deep caring, did evolve. Usually it's more like a family relationship, a closeness, yet separateness. My role as a sponsor always puts the relationship in jeopardy. It's my place to point out denial and danger. In friendship, it's not my job or responsibility to do that.

ED: I tell them to call me every day, to let me in on how they're feeling, just so I know. Sometimes they call, and sometimes they don't. I'm not looking to be their friend; I'm looking to help them work the steps. Yet, since all this is out of my hands, I have become good friends with a few of my sponsees. Sometimes I sponsor them. Sometimes they sponsor me. In fact, one of my sponsees is no longer my sponsee. He's my best friend.

You need more contact than just when the occasional tragic situations occur. You need everyday interactions in terms of who the person is and what makes them tick, because you'll find some very interesting things that occur in the process, you'll find ups and downs, and different qualities, and the reasons why they had problems. In the process of trying to find out why they had the problems, you find much of you interwoven.

LOIS: I don't see it as a friendship. I would in fact probably not sponsor someone who is already a friend. I see it as the sponsee wanting to get input regarding recovery from someone they admire. I do not ask or expect them to call me every day. Many of my sponsees have a lot of time in the program and call me when they have an issue to discuss. I do have a sponsee meeting once a month or so, so I get to see them even if I don't see them at meetings.

SUZANNE: It depends on the individual person. Sometimes people ask me to help them, and I want to be their friend. There are some who I have other things in common with, in addition to the fact that both of us are alcoholics, so over time, a friendship has developed. Other people who ask me to sponsor them have nothing in common with me, except the fact that we're alcoholics. So all I can really share with them is my experience of how I've been sober. That becomes more a relationship of meeting people at meetings and helping them go over their steps. I have never been somebody who has insisted that somebody call me every day. I find that most alcoholics don't take direction very well. And if somebody's nearly sober and vacillating and wondering whether they're alcoholic or not, that kind of expectation and pressure can be overwhelming. So I may make a suggestion that I'm available to them, and that if they like, they could call me, and it would probably be helpful for them if they checked in with me, at least on my machine, on a daily basis. But I don't insist upon it.

LEIGH: Fellowship is not friendship. Friends would let you get away with stuff the fellowship won't. Sometimes it's tricky. Especially with the love and the connection you make with your sponsee. It's a primary relationship that is not sexual. A sponsor has to tell you what to do. Sponsorship is not egalitarian. People get cocky and lose perspective of the dynamic. I've had it on both sides. I've had the focus on socialization rather than recovery. I really loved my sponsor in Amsterdam, but I had to terminate the relationship because it was not a working relationship. My needs were not being met.

BEA: I don't want to be their friend. I ran into problems with that. I found with my sponsor, she's like my big sister. I never hung out with her, but she was always there for me. I try to build confidence, because when we get to the Fourth Step, I want them to be as honest as they can be for themselves. So I'll try to build up the trust, but it's pretty much about going to meetings, coming over, doing step work, and not hanging out together. I don't like hanging out with my sponsees.

MARIASHA: My primary relationship is that of recovery and working the Twelve Steps. My goal is not to become friends, and that's caused problems in some of my relation-ships. Because of my life circumstances, I'm not as available as I think I could be, or should be, or would like to be. And since I've had a child, I've really limited the amount of sponsorship that I do. I have found it's a problem with spon-sees wanting more than I can give. When I was working, I worked sixty hours a week, leaving for work at ten in the morning and coming home at ten at night, six days a week. So I've had to make it very clear: if you're looking for a buddy, for a sponsor whose house you can just come over to and hang out at, for somebody you can drive around with and hang out with or go to meetings with, go get coffee with, or go to the movies with, that's not what I have to offer. My focus is getting together to do work.

DANNY: I try to develop a friendship. My first sponsor was somebody who I respected quite a bit. But, I didn't feel like it was a friendship-type relationship. It was sort of a supervisory relationship. I keep remembering my reluctance to get a sponsor, because I didn't want somebody telling me what to do. So, I try to be somebody they can trust, some-body they feel like they can just talk to, who happens to be their sponsor who gives them direction. As opposed to: I'm your sponsor, period. I know a lot of people don't want to get too close. But, I find sponsees take more chances when there's a bond between us. I don't spend a lot of time with them. One of my sponsees sings in a choir, and we hang out a little bit. We ride to meetings, and we talk about things besides recovery. I had another sponsee who was into music, and we went to see music together. Not a lot of socializing, but a lot of visiting.

DON: I will drop everything to hear someone's writing or step work, but I hate babies (sponsees) that just want to talk. I'm not a therapist. I have friends I talk to. They can get insulted if I'm not available for an hour or two. They need friends to interact with. I am friendly toward my babies, but I am not their friend. It always stays on the sponsor level—I'm the sponsor, you're the baby. My sponsor and I are not friends. He has his own friends. My sponsees should not be calling me that much—just with questions that pertain to sobriety. I try to stay detached from their drama and support their recovery.

MARGE: It is very intensive early and then gets less intensive, but all of my sponsor/sponsee relationships that are still ongoing have resulted in friendship. I have learned an incredible amount by experiencing the processes of my sponsees. A lot of them have made faster progress then I ever made, especially emotionally, because they have the emotional equipment when they get sober. I didn't. And they have the willingness that I didn't have. I learned a tremendous amount from their sincerity, directness, and honesty. I always try to share my mistakes, too. I learned that from Sara, who was soberly honest about herself. I was in despair the first three months I knew her. I was impressed that someone who was thirty years sober (which she was) was still doing some of the things a newcomer did. I thought she long since should've arrived at sainthood. But that was the most valuable thing because she was a person to me more quickly. I had a lot of trouble having her be a person to me, as she was older and a mother. I think it's inevitable at some point and time in the natural outgrowth that you become friends. There's not the heavy duty division anymore. I think people need sponsors or very honest friends in their entire lives. Whenever we're in the middle of a problem our perception is going to be clouded because we're coming from a painful place. Whomever it is, if they're looking at it from the outside and have an intimate relationship coupled with common sense and experience, has a clearer vision than you do. If you don't get that out of this program, you've missed something. That's the most valuable thing you can get—the ability to nonjudgementally observe your behavior in others before you act. I think we need a constant reminder of that.

WHAT IS FAIR FOR THE SPONSOR TO EXPECT FROM THE SPONSEE?

PATRICE: I ask them what they expect or need from me as a sponsor, what their definition of a sponsor is. Communication is a big part of good sponsorship, getting on the right page in the beginning really makes sponsoring easier. I also let them know I expect them to work harder at their recovery than I work at sponsoring them. I expect them to call me more than I'm calling them. After all it's their program not mine. I let them know I will support them, but I won't carry or chase them.

LOIS: I don't generally call my sponsees—of course I do sometimes, but I feel they should reach out for recovery, rather than me pushing it at them.

SUZANNE: I don't expect anything from anybody. The program is something everybody needs. People have to want it. And my experience with newcomers has been that to expect anything will only set you, as a sponsor, up for great disappointment, because sometimes people think they want to get sober, and they really don't. They're not willing to go to any lengths. So I expect nothing; I just try to share my experience, strength, and hope with people, and whatever happens, happens. And I really dissuade them in the very beginning from having me be like a sponsor-sponsor. I tell them I'll be a temporary sponsor, and we'll see how the relationship goes, see how it unfolds.

CHARLES: I ask them to come and be committed and to go to at least one meeting a day. I ask them to show up at a particular time and try to teach them commitment. When they say they'll be here at a certain time, I expect them to be on time. If they're not, I try not to make it mean anything, but just acknowledge that they weren't here on time. I try to teach them to do that with their sponsees. I think it's very important for them to have a three-ring notebook, sectioned off with at least eight dividers, to hold their notes, work from their steps, and so forth. That way, if they're having a problem, they can glance in there and see what they've done to work on that problem in the past.

LEIGH: I tell them: "This is about your recovery. My expectation is that you'll take responsibility and do the work. Are you willing to take direction? Do you want what I have?" Each person is different. I ask them, "What do you want from me?" I expect emotional honesty. I ask them, "Are you ready for this level of work?" I believe the first year is to learn how to be clean and work a program.

MARIASHA: I expect them to stay clean. If they don't stay clean, I don't continue to sponsor them because apparently what I'm doing isn't working for them. So I suggest they call me, and I will be supportive of them. I suggest they continue to look until they find somebody who they feel is giving them what they need to hear. I have not yet sponsored somebody that's relapsed. Other than that, I don't really expect anything. I'm not stringent in terms of how many meetings you've been to, how often you need to call me, or expecting you to write or read. I am not controlling in that regard. I'm more a resource, a source of support. Recovery has to be at their pace, not at my pace, so I don't give homework and deadlines.

DANNY: Initially, I don't tell them everything I expect of them. Basically, I let them know that if I'm going to sponsor them, it's their responsibility to call me. I expect them to follow those suggestions and to call me at least once a week. Although, I find myself not adhering to what I tell them, because I end up calling them. I tend to get really involved or try too much, but I like it. If they don't call me, I call them to see what's happening. Initially, that's what I expect. I don't jump into any writing and stuff in the beginning. I just want them to get comfortable and be able to get to know them first so I know how they react to certain things.

DON: I ask them, "What do you want to do? How can I help you?" I love babies (sponsees) who are willing to follow an example. I don't want ones who resist or are rebellious. I believe in "barefoot AA"—no frills, no BS, no fooling around. Don't snivel from the podium—speak with your sponsor.

MARGE: The meeting once a week is one; reading the book is another; the spiritual development is another, and I always tell people up front that I share with them what worked for me and, that at any time, if they don't think it's working for them, they need to tell me. I leave the relationship open, in the sense that I hardly ever require someone call me every day. If someone volunteers to do that, I'm perfectly okay with it. I tend to sponsor people who are pretty individual, not the run-of-the-mill folks. I find they're kind of like me: the bigger they are, the harder they fall. They have to have a really long leash in the beginning. I just try to let them know I'm there for them one hundred percent and want to do whatever I can to help them along in their program. I don't get into a lot of what their responsibility is because I think what worked for me was gentleness. There is always time to talk about what's not happening or what a problem is.

NATALIE: What do I expect of them? I expect them to be honest and be willing to take suggestions. Sponsees must be honest, open, and willing. I don't dictate their life. No judgements. I'm here to take them through the steps and guide them through difficult times. It's hard sometimes to have the patience to wait out the bad times, but the sun does come out. I also expect them to stay in touch, not just during the painful times, but through the good times, too. I do expect to develop a friendship, to bond. I care. If they're sincere, I care twenty-four hours a day.

BOB B.: The only expectation I have is to suggest they write, reflect, or come to some understanding on the first three steps. It's up to them to stay in contact; I'm not going to go chase everybody and try to contact them. If they want to get along with their recovery and want to get on to working some steps, it's necessary for them to do that first.

JEANETTE: They must be willing to go through the steps, along with a commitment to stay clean. Otherwise, I wouldn't give two cents for the way they feel.

BEA: I ask them what they expect from me first, what they're looking for in a sponsor, what they're looking for from me in particular. Then, I tell them what I expect from them. I expect them to work with me, to follow direction. When I give them writing assignments, and give them enough time, I expect them to do it. I expect them to be open, to try and build up some trust between them, to really start to trust me, and as we go on through the steps to nurture that. I have them call me every night in the beginning. When I ask someone to do something, I don't want to put something on them they can't do, and then they're going to feel bad about it. I want them to think about it. And if they're going to commit to doing it, I want them to do it.

KAREN: I tell newcomers what I expect: that they will follow direction and do the steps.

ED: I guess I expect them to want to change their lives. I tell them the way the sponsor/sponsee relationship works is by letting me get to know them and by them getting to know me. I may be the first person they've even considered trusting in years. I don't expect them to trust me at first. A sponsor is there to help you work the steps, because he's worked the steps. If a sponsee really uses me, calling me every other day, giving me the chance to draw on my experiences, forcing me to examine things that he doesn't understand, then I grow. We both grow. A sponsee gives me the chance to take everything I've learned in the rooms, mix it up with my life experiences, and then serve it up in such a way that I feel reborn. I come to believe all over again.

My sponsees keep me clean.

Chapter Four

Steps One, Two, and Three

- -

"I came to believe that we each have our own path, and that my job as a sponsor is not to get my sponsees to work the steps exactly as I did . . . but to discover their way to work the steps."

— ED

"I think that when people get their humanity, they get their higher power."

— CHARLES

Steps One, Two and Three. Should you start from the First Step regardless of how many steps your sponsee may have already worked? To write or not to write? How to help sponsees with their understanding of a Higher Power. Do you work the steps the same way with every sponsee?

....

This chapter focuses on the peripheral, but important, issues that come up around working Steps One, Two, and Three. No one likes to go back and do something over. A new sponsee may have recently completed a step and is looking forward to the next. Is it necessary to interrupt his or her progression and restart him or her on Step One or is it best to continue from where he/she is now?

Is it necessary or advantageous to write on the first three steps? It's commonly accepted to write on the First, but what about Steps Two and Three?

Can you help someone with something as personal as finding and defining his or her Higher Power? Hearing other people share in a meeting about their Higher Power can open new doors, but as a sponsor, are there particular things you can do to help this process?

Do you work the program the same way with each sponsee or do individual differences dictate how you give the program?

SHOULD YOU START FROM THE FIRST STEP REGARDLESS OF HOW MANY STEPS YOUR SPONSEE MAY HAVE ALREADY WORKED?

J.P.: Yes. Starting from Step One has been my own experience, so that's what I do. One reason I do it is because it's important I understand what kind of Higher Power you have. I also need to know that you have total trust in the program—to know that the Fourth Step will work.

M.T.: Emphatically yes! I made the mistake of not doing it with a woman I sponsored who was working what appeared to be a strong program. She was very involved in service, made lots of meetings and was also sponsoring other women. Her previous sponsor had moved away. But she didn't want to start over, even though she had just asked me to sponsor her and I had asked her to start at Step One. She was adamant that she didn't want to go back because she said it had taken her too long to get to where she was— at the Eighth Step. She said she loved her previous sponsor, and they had done good work together. I argued a little and then gave up. I figured it was her program, after all. I should have known when she showed up with her Eighth Step list on a piece of scrap paper (which she promptly proceeded to lose) that her program was none too great. Not wanting to be judgmental, I said nothing, and we proceeded to go over her Eighth Step list. It was hard because I knew virtually nothing about her family relationships and therefore, couldn't give her much guidance. As we went on to Step Nine, I tried to piece together what kinds of amends she should make. I asked about her relationships with the people on the list (her sister, father, etc.), which we had agreed was the way I would catch up. But it didn't work. For example, her sister reacted badly to her amends phone call, but I had no way of knowing what that meant. Was her amends complete anyway because she had called? Was her sister being unreasonable in her criticisms or was there more that needed to be done by my sponsee to make the situation right? How could I know with so little information? It turned out her sister's anger was justified and a phone call wasn't enough. I hadn't heard her Fourth Step so I had no idea of the history of the two. Later, there was a situation involving her mother and stepfather, and again, I had no clue what direction to give because I knew nothing about these people. They were perfectly hidden from me. This left a less than willing sponsee in control of information that would have enabled me to help her. I would never do it again. In fact, it turned out she did not have a good foundation in the other steps, just a superficial go at them. For example, she had decided as part of her program to diligently read the First Step every day—and had continued to do so at almost two years clean, though it had long before ceased to give her any real benefit. There were a lot of things that needed to be fixed in this woman's program of which I had no idea and only found out about in dribs and drabs. I don't care if the person is on her Twelfth Step (in which case, I might finish her up on it and start her again from Step One immediately), it is imperative she start from Step One with me, even if it is at an accelerated pace if she has done it before. With this sponsee, I even tried to get her to write on her powerlessness on another issue in her life (other than her addiction) so it would be a completely new application of the First Step, with the idea that we would move through the steps on that issue. When she was unwilling to proceed with it, it was time for an ultimatum—do the work or get another sponsor, which I wish I had said.

Starting from Step One is crucial. Each step builds on the other. The thought process that goes into this building is of key importance and you can only know what it is if you are present to hear it. I think the idea of doing the steps on another issue other than the core issue that brought the person into recovery is fine. Coming to believe on that issue, turning it over, and doing a Fourth Step and the subsequent steps are valid. Because everything is interrelated, it is inevitable that all the other issues and people in that sponsee's life will come in to play. With the sponsee I mentioned previously, I was trying to give her direction and it turned out she was giving me direction instead.

BEA: I've always gone to Step One, except with one girl. She was a friend and had some time. I didn't want to sponsor her, but we started at Step Eight. I'll never do it again. It was like she decided to be the sponsor. It was that one time I made that judgement. But now I'll always start from Step One. That's how I get to know somebody. If they don't share that stuff with me, I don't know who they are. And I don't know what we're working with.

BOB B.: Yes, I start them at the First Step. It's a basic lead into wherever they're going from there. It's not long and protracted. I think it's necessary to know that they've done that understanding or come to some conclusions about that before you proceed any further, even if they've done a fourth. The Fourth Step is only as much a matter of catching up on what's happening today as anything else. Because most of what's going on today is what happened yesterday anyhow.

SUNNY: I want to start from Step One. I want to get to know them. I want at least to have a Fourth Step from them. I like sponsoring people who have been in the program a while. If they're satisfied that they've taken the first three steps, then I'm satisfied. I do make step forms for Steps One, Two, and Three available to them.

PATRICE: I have no set pattern, except, if they are in a recovery home or recovery program, I want them to share their writings and steps with me, as well as their counselor. I also need to know their history and what their patterns of use were, their triggers (people, places, things). We go over their understanding of the steps and how they have worked them. If I'm comfortable with their understanding/knowledge, I will work with them at whichever step they're on. I really believe that you work the steps the rest of your life, but completing them the first time is very important. Lots of people get stopped in the program by their drive for perfection. If I miss something the first time, I can always catch it the second or third time. I'll never forget the feelings I had after my Fifth Step, and with each step it just increased: the feeling of being a part of, not just a hanger on. One of the true people in action, not just talking a program but doing it.

SUZANNE: I would say it depends on the individual person, and what's going on in her life. Some people need to do Step One a lot. Other people do Step One and may need to do Step Three or Step Four more. So for me it's a more individual experience. I will do it differently depending on what is going on with that sponsee. Some people are stuck in a lot of denial and rationalization about how manageable their lives were, so we'll work more on Step One. Some people are really clear about that, but they have no faith and trust, and so we work more on Step Three, to let go and give it to God and really expand the concept, or change their concept to a new concept. Others believe in God, have a really compassionate connectedness, but are totally unwilling to forgive themselves or accept they're human beings and have made mistakes. At that stage, we'll work more on Step Four. Some people have a great deal of difficulty taking responsibility for their behaviors, so we work on the steps that require making amends, asking for character defects to be removed, and promptly admitting being wrong when they're wrong. Still others can do all of that, but they're very selfish, self-absorbed, and self-obsessed, so they need to work more on being of service, Step Twelve. Some people don't have any experience of how to be still, how to pray, and how to meditate. Each person is so distinctly different, that even though each person has to do all of the steps, I think each of us has a place, developmentally, where we haven't expanded as much in a certain area. So I'll try to deal with that with each person.

ED: Yes and no. When I asked my sponsor to sponsor me, he asked me what step I was on. I said the Eighth Step, and we proceeded from there. So, if I get a new sponsee who has worked some of the steps and comes to me looking for direction on the next step, I'll give it. However, since the steps are more of a spiral than a circle, by the time we get to the Twelfth Step, it's time to start all over again, to take the time to reexamine the principles that we plan to practice in all our affairs.

I have been told that, for some people, to start all over again would feel like having their stripes pulled, negating all the work that had gone on before, so I don't. But, if someone asked me to, I would.

LOIS: I do not start from Step One with a new sponsee unless they request it. I start wherever they are.

LEIGH: Start from Step One—yes, absolutely. I need to get to know them, and they me. They start again from Step One if I'm sponsoring. If they just want some help with the steps, we move through them quickly. Basically, we have some discussion about their relationship with the steps so that I'm put in a position to give them advice.

DANNY: I go through them, but not like they have to work them all over again. For those who have gone to a recovery house and worked the first three or four steps there, I let them know that if I'm going to sponsor them, we will do it a little differently and a little slower than they did in recovery house. There, they usually rush through the steps. Even though they have answered the questions in the hospital, it's not working the steps. I told one sponsee: "When I feel like you've internalized the steps, we'll move on."

MARIASHA: Yes, in the form of a review. I won't necessarily go back and have somebody do a Fourth, or work through the steps in-depth. But I need to know who they are. I do ask them to write an abbreviated version of the first three steps. How it was for them in terms of their disease, and how it is for them today. How those same concepts apply to their life today in recovery, as compared to how they apply in relation to the disease. In terms of having them do a Fourth and a Fifth with me, I don't have them do formal ones, but I do ask them to give me enough background so I have a context in which to understand them. If I don't know what their issues are, if I don't know about their family background or about the traumas and the experiences that they've had, I don't have a context in which to understand the problems they're having or to give them any kind of an insight into what I think might be going on, or what the defect or the shortcoming is that they might be going through. I only ask them to bring me up to speed, but they don't have to do a formal Fourth and Fifth with me.

LISA: No. It really depends on where the person is when I get them. If somebody has just finished writing up a Fourth Step, is ready to dump their Fifth Step, and had a problem with their sponsor, I would feel like it would be very dangerous to try and send that person back to Step One. It really depends on where the person is.

MARGE: Yes, in the sense that I really want to know whether they have grasped and internalized the concept of their powerlessness over alcohol. Not that they're an alcoholic, that they have a label, but that they are actually powerless over alcohol. And then, if they are powerless, what they're convinced will help them in that regard. The way it was put to me was that if we're powerless over alcohol, if that's simply the truth, then to try to fight off alcohol by ourselves is an insane approach doomed to failure. Therefore, we need something else to provide an answer to that. In AA, that something else is God, as it says in the *Big Book*. The answer to that situation is simply to surrender any control we think we have over drinking and using to God and allow that control to rest in God and not in the individual. Then, we have simply given that problem away. It is not part of our context anymore. In my experience, this is the only freedom; this is the freedom that the AA program provides. It talks about it in the book, about the problem simply being removed and placed in a position of neutrality, safe and protected. The only way I know to get there is to go through those first three-step processes and to surrender your disease and keep it surrendered. Therefore, achieve that state of grace with all those benefits.

NATALIE: I don't force the steps down their throat. I try to find out why they want to change their lives, which is Steps One and Two. The Third Step can be done in the desert or in a living room. I did mine on the corner of Santa Monica and San Vicente Boulevards (in Los Angeles). The bus was coming. I said "God" and the Third Step prayer. There was a feeling that washed over me, like a cup was being filled. I felt a spiritual change right then.

I have them do it just the way the *Big Book* says. It's a

simple program; don't complicate it. No essays on the step, just talking about them is fine. I tell them to underline anything they don't understand. I suggest they make book and step study meetings and have a dictionary handy when they're reading.

TO WRITE OR NOT TO WRITE?

KAREN: I always begin by having them write on Step One. I tell them to cite ten very specific examples of how drug or alcohol use has adversely affected their lives, not just, "Alcohol makes me lose my temper," but "There was one time I had a fight with my boyfriend and put my fist through the window. I had to get stitches in my arm, where I now have a scar, and had to pay for the broken window, even though I couldn't afford it at the time. I always thought it was his fault this happened, because he was such a jerk. But when I'm really honest about it, it happened because I was drunk and out of control."

PATRICE: I believe in writing! It helps people get in their reality in a more complete/concrete way. By my writing the steps and going over them with my sponsor I began to not only understand them, but to really believe that, indeed, I had taken the steps and could then hold my own in any meeting discussion without being overpowered by someone else's understanding or way of doing the steps. I have sponsored people that have learning disabilities and aren't able to write. In those cases I have them use a tape recorder, going through the steps just like they would if they wrote them out. Also, I've worked with some who are able to read but unable to write due to their inability to spell (if they can read their own spelling, this doesn't apply). I or someone else acted as their secretary and did the writing for them. This takes a special talent to do because you have to be able to do it without influencing or changing any of their words.

SUZANNE: I like people to write; however, a lot of people aren't capable of writing. They don't have the skills to do it. Because they haven't had the education, they're not capable of writing; it brings up tremendous anxiety. When people can, I prefer to have them write, because I think it's much more meditative and contemplative for people to write. If they can't, I will talk with them about it, discuss it, and have a conversation.

MARGE: I don't have them write on Steps One, Two and Three unless they insist. I think it's more of an ongoing internal surrender process. I don't find value in knowing the patterns of my drinking. I don't find value in knowing what might be the causes of my drinking. The only thing I find value in writing about might be to come to "I'm powerless over alcohol," if that's necessary. I think surrendering your drinking to your Higher Power is the spiritual leap that requires a willingness to do that and a willingness to be placed in a position where you simply couldn't drink even if you wanted to. Unless someone is willing to make that leap, it's not going to happen. I don't think any amount of writing is going to convince someone that is the thing to do. I think it's a positive, voluntary thing, rather than doing it out of fear of whatever might happen over here. I think until you can turn that around internally, you simply cannot take that step, because it's a joy step.

M.T.: I have sponsees write on all the steps. It's too easy to have some amorphous experience if you're just talking about it. Writing makes everything clearer, more concrete. You get to see what you really think when you write it down not just what you *think* you think. I find that happening now, writing my answers to these questions.

CHARLES: We write on all the steps, or most of the steps. Particularly, we write on the First Step in-depth. We write about what their drinking history is. I let them discuss that with me for twenty minutes before they start writing.

I don't think any person that I've ever sponsored can work a Fourth Step or a First Step without me. I don't care what people say. I don't think any sponsee is capable of writing without help from their sponsor. They need direction. And if that sponsor's been sponsored, he knows how to write. I definitely know how to get most of the information out of them within thirty-five minutes. We don't write for days. We write for thirty-five minutes at a time, and then we talk. I can get most problems assessed within thirty-five minutes, maybe twenty, if they're really not thinking, just writing. If you get a sponsee who thinks too much, it will take longer.

First of all, if you're in the program of AA, and you're showing up to meetings, you've done part of Step One, because you're there. You've changed; you're listening. Sometimes there is writing in Step Two, especially about their concept of God. I try to find out what their concept of God was before they got to me and before they got to the program. I ask them what their ideal God would be. I let them write that and then look and think about that a little bit, not digest it. Next, I tell them who their ideal God is and could be is not the one they're serving, if they have one at all. It also brings God to their consciousness. There are a lot of things they think of in their heads, in their subconscious, that won't be in their consciousness. I think if they talk about it and get it into a conversation, they can, finally, after three, four, or six months or even a year, have a pretty good concept of what God is.

LISA: Yeah, usually I do. Most always.

BOB B.: I have them write on Steps One, Two, and Three, even if it's just a reflection, a digestion, or some kind of understanding as to where they're coming from.

I might ask one to write on the person or on a resentment. I might tell another to put it on tape; he may not be capable of writing that type of thing. Sometimes it's just a matter of working that thing by understanding, in a discussion with the person. Or sometimes I come across a person and discuss what he is reading and his comprehension of it. I had difficulty in that area because words changed in my head, meanings changed. I didn't fully understand certain things that were being said. Sometimes we need to sit down and talk about the definitions of what you're thinking. Things need to be looked at in terms of comprehension, understanding, or background. I think you have to be open to different methods: going the same direction, doing the same thing, but using different methods than usual to obtain that. It becomes necessary to be creative.

BEA: I have a little format I use for the first four steps, and most of the time I hand that out. We work it over together. There have been a couple of times where, because of who the girl was or what she needed, I just had her free write, not telling her what to do, just asking her to sit down and start writing. But, most of the time, I do a format.

J.P.: I explain that I come from the "write your steps" school. The First Step is on me! I help them with it. Any advancement is on them. They need to come to me and say, "I'm ready for the Second Step."

DANNY: Sometimes I have them list the things that make them powerless. I don't have them all write on Steps One, Two, and Three because to me those are steps that you have to live. I have them describe their Higher Power to me. We discuss any previous religious background. We have long discussions about the difference between religion and spirituality, because some of them immediately say, "I've always believed in God. I was raised in the church." Sometimes I have them write a little bit on the First Step, in terms of ways they see their will and ways they can change their behavior by doing God's will.

It's been an individual thing. With most of my sponsees, I've had them do some writing on the First Step, more of a list actually, so that they can understand their powerlessness in recovery. I have them write about things during the week that they're powerless over, even if it's just a word. Rather than try to do paragraphs of writing, I keep it real simple: words, people, or events that make them feel powerless. Then we talk about it.

JEANETTE: The first time you go through the steps with a sponsee you're winging it. Really, newcomers are admitting themselves to you. You don't want to be too judgmental—that's not why they're doing it. You try to give unconditional love to help them get through their first years. I think it's a good idea to write Steps One and Two. One page each. Not a lot.

DO YOU WORK THE SAME WAY WITH ALL OF YOUR SPONSEES?

DON: I have an individual approach with each one: get to know them and see what each one needs. "Let's find out about you." I modify my instructions all the time. Each sponsee is an individual, based on their personality. Some come into the program very surrendered and don't need me to do Steps One through Three with them. If they're unsure about their alcoholism, if they're waffling, than they write it. I don't do everyone the same, but I do require that they work the steps.

ED: I always start out with a pre-step piece to get them thinking about how they might want to work the steps, to try and get them to commit to working the step with me. If they commit, we proceed.

I work most of the steps the same way with most of my sponsees. With the Fourth Step, however, I use the NA guide; I think that it is a very loving and caring piece of program literature. So do some of my sponsees. Many things were revealed as I worked my way through the guide. But others panic when they see all the topics and breakdowns, so I use a simple table I picked up from an AA seminar I attended in New York. It uses the idea that an inventory is just a list. It helps you to make lists.

I came to believe that we each have our own path, and that my job as a sponsor is not to get my sponsees to work the steps exactly the same way I did, but to discover their way to work the steps, a way to make the steps their own. The steps have to take root in our hearts, through our experiences, until, little by little, they become part of our life, become our first reaction. I guess I came to believe that people are inherently good, that their true nature is a loving, kind, and compassionate nature that using just clouded.

PATRICE: Almost the same, but some are ready for the *Big Book* method and some aren't. But they all do written steps, even the ones with learning disabilities, only they do it with a partner who acts as a secretary taking dictation. Most people do better with step guides that ask questions.

DANNY: At this point, I don't work the same way with each one. For example, one of my sponsees has a learning disorder. As for his "writing," we do most everything orally. I got him the *NA Basic Text* on tape, and we listen to that. When they pass out the things at meetings, he'll take something to read, but I help him on almost every other word. So I don't push him to write. It varies from person to person, based on the time that sponsees have, they are all at different levels in their step recovery.

MARIASHA: I work the steps the same way with each sponsee.

BEA: Yes. If they're not in a recovery house, then we just go on through the steps. I really keep them a long time on Steps One, Two, and Three. It could be six months— two months for each step. I really want them to internalize the acceptance, the trust. I'm not going to let anyone do a Fourth Step with me if I don't think they trust me, because then it's like defeat. It's wasting my time, it's wasting their time. So, I try to build up that confidence, that trust, for them, so they can tell me whatever they have to tell me. It just works so much better that way.

MARGE: No. I do work them differently. What I know to be true on every level for me is not what I pass on about the steps. I have found that sponsorship is the one place where, although I have strong opinions, I have been able to really surrender whatever it is I think needs to be accomplished and allow God to guide that process. Then, and when I speak, are the two times when I've really been able to let go of the little ''I.'' The rest of the time, it's a real argument. But I really think that's an intuitive process. That's what's marvelous about it, what provides both sponsor and sponsee with the ongoing spiritual experience in their relationship. I would hope I could only improve and never get out of that, because it's one of the memories I have of the Fifth, Sixth, and Seventh Steps. And in those experiences, they are probably the most precious memories I have sober.

CHARLES: Yes, I do work with all my sponsees the same way. They have to go to three or four meetings a week. That's definite. When sponsees don't go to more than three meetings, I don't think their progress is rapid. I think if they go to more meetings, they do more, they become sponsors more quickly. Once they start reading the *Big Book*, once they start reading the steps, and once they start working the steps, they have to go to a step meeting every week, all the sponsees do.

If I have a sponsee that's sponsoring other people, the way I sponsor him is totally different than if he's not working with sponsees. When my sponsees have sponsees, they're calling me a lot of times to ask me what I do about certain things. We are on the same level; we're working together to solve some problem. It's not just my experience on that problem. It becomes more like, "I never did that. That's good." I get to see my suggestions and my experience work in them, then come back as a different experience, which we can take to a third person.

I think that everybody is different, but the primary problems are there, usually. I think in most cases the primary problems are unresolved relationships with their parents or whoever raised them. So I'd like to go and settle that and get that going.

KAREN: I work the steps basically the same with each sponsee; what may differ is the length of time it takes to reach each one and go through it.

BOB B.: I think sponsees, like sponsors, have certain capabilities, certain abilities. So, very often, we have to be novel enough to shift and change in terms of what they are doing. It may be the same thing but done a different way.

M.T.: Yes, because I take each sponsee through the steps as I understand them, giving them direction based on the aspects that I think are important to focus on. The steps are the steps and represent truth which is unchanging. The information I give my sponsees is the truth about the steps as I have experienced it and understand it. What I tell them to write or read or look into is based on that. The information I have to give doesn't change from person to person.

HOW DO YOU HELP SPONSEES WITH THEIR UNDERSTANDING OF A HIGHER POWER?

J.P.: I've found through experience with sponsees that those who readopt their religion, who embrace the religion of their upbringing again, relapse and don't come back. I've had six who have done that. It's crucial that your Higher Power is loving, and you feel that. We need love in our life.

You can't alter the program to fit your life.

It's important to commune and speak to your Higher Power once a day in one way, shape, or form. I tell my sponsees that they must make an effort to alter their body position, to humble themselves before something that is greater than they are. They call on this power many times in their life. It deserves their humility.

I have many Catholic resentments from my own experience with it. I try my hardest not to let them out—not to impose these views on my sponsees.

SUZANNE: I have conversations with people about that,

whether it's an old idea of a God that's limited and comes from an old belief that needs to be expanded or changed, or whether they've created a new idea that's more supportive of a real personalized connectedness.

M.T.: I think it's key to tell them how I came to believe and what I came to believe, to check their progress with the Second and Third steps and to let them know it gets clearer and stronger as you continue on the path. If I had stayed on the Second Step until I fully believed, I'd still be there at nine years. What I came to believe, at first, was that I could get clean (which I never believed before I came to NA), and from there that there was a loving force at work in my life, even if it was generated by my good energy increasing the longer I stayed clean and practiced the spiritual principle of the program. There has to be the willingness to have faith and to trust others' experience as something you can own, too. I think it's key to have involvement with sponsees' Second and Third Steps. If they can't suspend negative judgement long enough to have faith or if they harbor so many reservations about the validity of these crucial steps, they won't feel safe doing a Fourth on any deep level, and the future steps will be compromised. Having a good foundation here is key.

BEA: That's a good question. I guess I just try to keep it real simple, introduce some kind of spirit or Higher Power on a very physical level in the beginning. Not me. That's not what I'm talking about. I mean the group. If they're in a recovery house, the recovery house. Something that is keeping them clean until they can find something inside. I've got quite a few books that tie in spiritually with the steps. We'll go through this book, *Serenity*, that has the steps and breaks them down, looking at them spiritually. I ask them to pray. I ask them to pray in the morning; I ask them to pray at night; I ask them to pray for things they need specifically, whether it's willingness or discipline . . . whatever it is they need, just so they can focus on their deficiencies. If they focus on it, they'll be able to see the changes more. I'll try to get them to go to a spiritual meeting once a week. I guess really what I do is show them how I see God working in my life, pass that on to them, and try to point out when I see God working in their lives, to help them become aware of it.

LEIGH: I pass on the idea of a loving, caring, nurturing Higher Power. I stay on the Third Step until they understand. I focus on the little miracles. One man worked for two years on his Third Step. He couldn't believe in God. I had him pray to my God. He believed I believed in God. I had him pray, "Dear God, even though I don't believe in you, will you help me anyway?"

DANNY: I have an analogy that I use about when I learned to float and I couldn't do it. It was because I wasn't surrendering. I found there's a part in the Second Step that talks about the fact that there's a void, and we surrender to our disease, and we stop using. I tend to tell them it's not some mysterious thing out there, it's within them. It's been there since they were born. It's something we lose connection with when we put drugs in our bodies. Drugs shut off that spiritual connection. There's this thing that knows the difference between right and wrong and cares about people. That's part of the Higher Power. It's the way babies look at you, the openness they have. I tell them if they have to use the examples that are given, using the group as a Higher Power or using somebody else's Higher Power, that's okay. Eventually, once they identify the qualities they want in their Higher Power, they can start to trust this thing that has those qualities and cares about them. And, it's about doing the next right thing. As long as they keep doing that, they start to get that contact.

Several of the guys that I sponsored had religious backgrounds, and one of them wanted to go back to church. I said, "That's okay, but what we're talking about is separate from that." I also tell them all about my Higher Power and try to get them to try to see the difference. I usually start by saying, "Whether you believe it works, or whether or not you believe in a Higher Power, I want you to pray to have the obsession to be lifted." After five or six years of coming to meetings, I decided to try it, and it worked. That gave me the faith in the possibility that it was a Higher Power acting in my life, because this thing went away. From then on I started believing in the concept. I don't push them to the Second Step, but I try to show them as many times as possible how their Higher Power is working as their lives progress. They see examples of change, and then they come to believe.

JEANETTE: I only help them with their understanding of a Higher Power if I'm asked. They should be praying and meditating.

PATRICE: I have sponsees write about what God has been to them, what they have been taught, what they like or dislike about that. Then they write all the possibilities that a Higher Power could be or not be to them: what do they want to call it, etc.

LISA: I usually ask them what they would like their Higher Power to be. And I share. Mostly, I share my experience with a Higher Power.

MARIASHA: I help them come to their own understanding. I share my own struggle, what my questions were, what my concerns were, and how I reconciled them. I try to listen to them and the baggage they brought in with them, and try and help them find their own solutions. I ask that they make an effort to connect with people who they identify with and feel some sort of connection with, and ask them to share. Ask those people to share with them how they worked it through so that maybe they can benefit from the experience of numbers, rather than just me. I sponsor women from different faiths and within the same faith; we all have our own feelings about Higher Power, good and bad. I think you have to be very individual.

BOB B.: I think that's a very difficult thing, because I think they should have to come to their own concept as to what a Higher Power is. I think each person has to seek his own direction or own path in terms of his Higher Power. I might confuse him with mine or my lack of one, or whatever the case might be. I think it's a matter, at some point, of acknowledging who is doing things. It becomes some kind of understanding of some ultimate power you experience and that becomes a part of your understanding, rather than my understanding or somebody else's. Very often it is a case of finding spiritual readings or spiritual teachings. They stim- ulate the mind and your thinking. Many truisms come out of them. You are able to respond in a certain way and to come to some understanding of what's happening in your life and what's happened in other people's lives. I try not to be directive in that respect. I try not to say, "I go to church over here," or "I do this over there."

ED: I don't. I listen. I let them know how I struggled with the Higher Power, with the word "God," and with control issues. But I always end up turning back to them and telling them they have to struggle with this themselves;

they have to come to an understanding of *their* Higher Power, *not mine*.

When I first came around, I borrowed other people's Higher Powers and tried to make them mine; it seemed to work for a while, but they always left me at some point where I knew it was a lie. I couldn't believe anymore. So I had to go and find my Higher Power.

SUNNY: As far as helping them with their understanding of a Higher Power, I tell them how I came to it, which was very difficult. My husband was an atheist and if he hadn't stayed, I wouldn't have either. The easiest answer for me is, I can't find God, so I'll let God find me. This year it's God in me. The God in me salutes the God in you.

CHARLES: I think when people get their humanity, they get their Higher Power. I think you can also get your spirituality or your God concept by working for/with others, by being committed and being there and not knowing why. If I can find sponsees who will go and get out of themselves and be there for somebody else, just be in a commitment, they can get their humanity and their God from that. I think that's how it comes for most of us. I don't think it's a flash in the pan or a lightening bolt. There are those spiritual awakenings.

Chapter Five

Steps Four and Five

"I think the Fourth Step comes up naturally when people start to realize that how they're trying to live their life now is in conflict with how they lived their life before."

— MARGE

Steps Four and Five. How do you gauge when it's time for sponsees to write their Fourth Step? What direction can you give? What is your part, as a sponsor, in doing a Fifth Step?

Writing a fearless and searching moral inventory, as the Fourth Step requires, is generally considered a recovery accomplishment. Many people feel the awareness they had before writing one and the awareness they have after are hard to compare. And the bond they have with their sponsor is greatly strengthened by completing the process in the Fifth Step. But, some people write their Fourth Step in their first three months, while others haven't written one with three years in recovery. Does it matter when a person writes it? Should when to write a Fourth Step always be left up to the sponsee? Do they always know when it's time to do it? Or is it a sponsor's responsibility to determine that?

Everyone knows a sponsee's responsibility in doing a Fifth Step— show up with the Fourth and be ready to go over it — it's stated in the step itself. But a Fifth Step takes two to complete. What then is the sponsor's part? Is it an active or passive role? Some sponsors instinctively know how to make the most of the process and others don't, especially if they didn't have a particularly great experience when they did their own. Depending on the situation, just listening may be the only thing needed, but here are some other ideas for your participation as a sponsor to give (and get) the most in an important recovery experience.

How do you gauge when it's time for sponsees to write their fourth step?

JEANETTE: You can't stop everything until the Higher Power concept is good. Many times doing a Fourth Step will help sponsees gain a better spiritual understanding of their Higher Power. By and large, the first inventory is very shallow. The Fourth Step is going to be required whenever you're in pain.

LISA: How do I judge when it's time for sponsees to start? When I feel like they have definitely made a decision to go on with the rest of the steps, when I feel like they have a good grasp of Steps One and Two and they've made a decision. If you waited for everybody to totally turn their will and their lives over, you'd have a lot of people on Step Three for the rest of their lives.

Do I put a time limit on it? Yes. When I have somebody start writing their Fourth Step, I usually make an appointment within a week of when I think they'll be ready to do their Fifth Step.

PATRICE: The best thing to do after completing your Third Step is to go directly into your Fourth Step. I believe that in the beginning there's a lot of grief work, losses, etc. and doing the Fourth Step helps to not only access that grief but start the healing process. I've seen people put their Fourth Step off. They end up suffering through a lot of the same behaviors, only this time without the benefit of drugs to take away or numb the pain. Some people have such a high tolerance for intolerable behavior (their own and others'), along with an addiction to drama, that they stay in it for years or go back out. Dr. Bob and Bill W. did all the steps while still detoxing from their last drink. That's not what I did or recommend, but I do keep that in my conversation with people I sponsor.

KAREN: I gauge their readiness to do a Fourth Step based on how thoroughly I feel they've worked through the first three steps. The people I've sponsored have been anxious to get started on their Fourth Step, though I think it makes everyone nervous. That nervousness has to be evaluated as normal, though. Otherwise, if the fear is too great, I'd wait long enough for them to lay down more of a foundation before starting, but I'd have to be sure it wasn't just about avoidance. I had a sponsee go out and use the night we began to talk about the Fourth Step. I think she chose to do so, and it wasn't because of the Fourth Step. But perhaps waiting until the obsession has been lifted is the best rule of thumb.

NATALIE: I don't gauge. Sponsees know when it's time. They feel it. If they're going through a situation, I'll say maybe it's time, but I don't judge or point a finger. If it's someone with time, I'll be more blunt. Often I'll say, "If you don't want to sit in the pain, here's a step you can use." But I'm not a "step Nazi." I believe honesty is very important and if you don't clear away the wreckage of your past, it will cause you to use. I believe that drug addicts have a harder time than alcoholics because the denial with drugs is deeper. If they don't do a Fourth Step, their sobriety can lose its priority.

M.T.: I think, unless there are extenuating circumstances (i.e., the sponsee is extremely fragile and needs time to build self-esteem or she will only beat herself up with the Fourth Step findings), sponsees should start their Fourth Step after they've done their Third. I always suggest they start one when I feel that they've got a good grasp of the Third Step, and, unless they convince me otherwise, I except them to embark on it right away. I have no problem with a sponsee staying on the Third Step for however long it takes to make that Higher Power connection. But once it's made, it's time for action.

In the NA step book, *It Works How and Why*, they say, based on the fellowship's experience, "Sooner or later those who don't work this crucial step relapse." I believe that is true. When we look at the overall low success rate of people getting and staying clean, we realize how truly difficult it is to stay clean/sober/abstinent, etc. Consequently, the less you do, the likelier you are to fail. Personally, I wouldn't go out of my way to hang out with people with three, four, or five years clean in the program who haven't written a Fourth Step. My description of "winners" are those striving for the spiritual awakening talked about in the Twelfth Step. Anyone really seeking one would want to do a Fourth as soon as possible. Also, the Fourth Step alleviates a lot of fear that for me wasn't dismissed any other way. Trying to work on character defects without a Fourth Step behind you doesn't make sense. There's no time limit on working steps, of course. I practice them all—but I have worked them all. To me, it's a fragmented program if you take a year or more break after a Third Step. To me, when they say "sooner or later," I think later is too late.

I think a month is plenty to write a Fourth, but it seems all of my early sponsees took many months to do theirs (which I now see was procrastination). So now, I like to set a date to do the Fifth at the same time they're starting a Fourth (someone once told me it was a sure way to get one done) so it's not open-ended. I always tell sponsees this is the first of many they will write, and for me that has been true. Nothing shows me what's going on like a Fourth Step, and nothing made me feel more a part of the program than taking that concrete and dramatic action. I did one on relationships (I highly recommend it as a subject for a Fourth Step) and, even though I had covered relationships in my first Fourth Step, when I later focused only on that topic, much more was revealed. We come into the program with so much baggage and continue to carry it until we do a Fourth Step. The Fourth Step is the first time we're asked to examine what we've done and what we're doing (character defects at work). So until we do one, we're still operating on old stuff, and we're prevented from moving forward. I believe the program is accomplished through being of service and working the steps. If you hold up on a Fourth Step, you're holding up on all the steps that come after it as well as all the rewards they hold—the freedom from bondage. The Twelve Steps are a program of liberation. If you stop after Three, you're just staying bound by all the trash you carried around in addiction. You may have hope and have made new friends, you have the rooms to vent and share in, but for me there's no real progress as it's laid out in the steps, if the next step isn't worked promptly after the previous one is understood and being practiced. And if these programs are about anything, they're about change.

MARGE: I think the Fourth Step comes up naturally when people start to realize that how they're trying to live their life now is in conflict with how they lived their life before. There's some kind of process that goes on that lets everybody know some of those things have to be neutralized before they can go on. Usually, that's pretty obvious. From what I've observed, it's been between seven and nine months of sobriety when that comes up. Usually my people will volunteer then, but if not, I volunteer it for them. I don't necessarily put a time limit on it, but I think a month is sufficient time. Usually people are through before then, or they're procrastinating. So, we talk about what they can do to help themselves out. I've put time limits on it before, in the sense of saying "next Friday night." And we just wind it up.

ED: My sponsor feels that people should go through the steps as soon as possible, so that they'll know what people are talking about when they hear about the steps. When sponsees are done with the first three steps, it's time to move on to the Fourth. It takes as long as it takes. I have no time limit, but I'll ask them how they're doing, and remind them why they're doing this step, and urge them not to let it die.

LOIS: I don't really give them orders or time limits. I feel it's my job to make suggestions, and then it's the work I do on myself to let go of the results.

LEIGH: I don't believe in doing a Fourth Step right away. I can't make rules for everybody, and I'm not God. I sponsored a Bowery bum who had an incest issue. I suggested he didn't deal with it in his first year. He said he had to deal with it. I asked my sponsor what to do. My sponsor said, "How do you know what he needs? Are you God? Just give him love." Now I just try to be present and available to hear what they need. Only they can tell me. If you work the program, it will work for you. I do believe in recommending therapy if someone needs it. Things will start to come up. I prefer that my sponsees have one year clean before doing a Fourth Step. I tell them to do it as quickly as they can, say two weeks. I check in with them. It's okay if it takes a month. I've done Fifth Steps with partial Fourth Steps and then done it again when it was finished. It doesn't need to be perfect, you just need to move on. You'll do more later. I've found if people write for too long they are not saying anything new.

BEA: How do you gauge when it's time? It depends on whether or not somebody is in a recovery house. If she is in a recovery house, there is a little more of a time limit. Usually, I give sponsees about two to three weeks on each of the first three steps, working with me. Then, we go right into a Fourth Step. Sometimes not enough has come up for the person, but that's okay; she will do another eventually anyway, sooner or later. If they're not in a recovery house, I don't put time limits on, unless I see they're avoiding it. In that case, I tell them, "We need to set something more constructive, more definite, because it's not working like this." With when to finish, I try to be very flexible, because it needs to work in their lives. I want them to do it. I don't want them to not do it and feel bad. I may say, "Three weeks. That gives you two weekends, plus some time in between." If they are still really having a hard time with it, I don't come down real hard on them. I just try to work with them, because there's probably a reason why they're having difficulties with it. I don't think there's a definite time that somebody has to do a Fourth Step; it's just as things come up. I do set time limits, but very flexible ones, that are very easy to meet.

DANNY: When I feel like they understand the Third Step and they're living it, I usually give them the Fourth Step guide and tell them I want them to read the Fourth Step a few times. Don't write anything, just read through it and get comfortable with the concept. If there's a step study meeting where they are speaking on the Fourth Step, I'll tell them to look out for that. I don't put a timeline on it.

In my opinion, the people that have a hard time with the Fourth Step are people who have rushed through the first three and don't have a solid foundation. They don't have the trust and the faith that things are okay today. So when they go delving into the past, they get frightened. Fear is one of our biggest enemies. It's really about being comfortable with who you are today, doing the first three steps and then moving into Step Four. For me, the first three steps have been such a maintenance thing in my daily life that I try to get sponsees to that point before we start doing this other in-depth stuff.

MARIASHA: The Fourth and the Fifths that I've heard have been at my sponsees' own choice, when they've said they were ready. We've talked about it, we've gone through the steps at a pace that I let them determine. I might make a suggestion, or I might say, "I think you might benefit . . ." or "It seems like you have a foundation of the first three steps, and it might be beneficial for you if you were to pursue the Fourth." They have a foundation; they've got some time; they've been clean for awhile, that's basically the gauge. I don't encourage an individual to jump into writing a Fourth Step. It's a relative term. Early in recovery, I don't give direction; I make suggestions. I get my cues from the people that I work with. I think there's a qualitative difference between doing something when you feel ready and prepared to take on that commitment and doing it because of some kind of an external obligation. So I don't set the pace for recovery. I'm just a guide. If I feel like somebody is procrastinating, I might make a suggestion, point that out, or share my own experience with my own reluctance of what I went through. My sponsor never pressured me. She was just there for me when I decided it was time. So, I try to model that with my sponsees.

It's somebody else's direction if they tell you to do a Fourth Step, because they think it's the right time. You will not benefit from it because your heart isn't in it. Working recovery houses, I have seen that happen time and time and time again, where they're not equipped spiritually or psychically to cope with what they unearth. Or they're so blocked because they don't have enough recovery within them and enough willingness that they're not going to have the recall to write a Fourth Step anyway. So my belief is the old cliche: you can guide a horse to water, but you can't force him to drink. You can be ten years clean and not have done an inventory. The measure of spirituality and spiritual growth that people live by, to the extent that the spiritual principles are working in their lives and they've experienced some peace, joy, and happiness, is relative to the amount they participate. Maybe they've done a Fourth, maybe they haven't. I have heard people share that they don't believe in God, and they've never done a Fourth Step. They've got as much or close to as much time as I have. Who am I to judge the measure of their recovery and how close or how far away they are from relapse? I've been clean for thirteen years, but I didn't do an inventory until I had two years clean. So was I at risk? Possibly. I'm still at risk, and I've done one. I believe it's the extent to which you participate in your program, not whether you've done a Fourth, that determines whether you're going to stay clean. There are people who do Fourths and are extremely shallow, and they don't gain any insight, don't benefit doing a Fourth except maybe they've purged themselves of some of their truths. And there are people who do Fourths that are really searching, fearless, moral inventories. They really benefit; it's extremely therapeutic to reality test with another human being. So I try not to judge. Personally, I would never say to a sponsee, "You've been clean for three years, and you haven't done a Fourth. I think you're at risk of relapse." I might say, "You need to look at the relationship between the degree of madness and discomfort you're experiencing and the fact that you haven't been willing to do that. You haven't been willing to reveal yourself, to take risks, and to gain some insights into the dynamics of your problems. It might be beneficial for you if you were to take a Fourth so you could learn. You could apply the knowledge from having done a Fourth."

BOB B.: Much has to do with where the person is in terms of growth period: Are they hung up on not finishing Steps One, Two, and Three, or do they have no understanding of Steps One, Two, and Three? Until you get a good grasp of One, Two, and Three, going on to Four would only be premature. Because I think you need an understanding of the reason for the first three steps. For some it takes longer than others to achieve that understanding. I think you have to feel like that is what's needed; it's not something someone can tell you. There's no time element involved. It has a lot to do with each person going at his own speed. When it starts causing difficulty from not doing it, when a person reaches that particular point, you almost know that's what's necessary, that's what's going to help. Then, they need to go about the business of doing it: sit down, pencil in hand, start the process, and do something. It's not a matter of finishing that's always hard. Some might do it in bits and pieces.

Life is problematic. I think you need to be looking at some of those areas of concern. On a daily basis, you may have to do a Tenth Step and write about it. You have to look at it, see what the patterns are, see where they're reoccurring. I think a person will find the good results, and then they get by that spot. Next, you encourage them into some other areas that need to be worked. I don't know if there's any time limit. I don't have a particular time limit, no schedule. The urgency is how fast you want to recover. If you want to recover at a slow rate, great. These are the things you have to do. Don't get too fast, then you don't let them finish. That becomes important.

J.P.: I sponsor twelve guys now, some with over three years clean. I've never heard a Fifth Step. I have four guys writing a Fourth, but I believe that people work through it in their own time. I will not force a sponsee to work a step because I'm on a time table, because I'm not. Often, those people who call with problems have those problems because they're not working a step. I tell them the problems will not begin to disappear on their own; they will begin to disappear when these people do a Fourth Step.

Sometimes I do feel like a failure for not having heard Fifth Steps. But then I remember it took me two years to

do my Fourth Step. It travelled with me to three countries
and eighteen states! My sponsor allowed me the latitude to
realize that I needed to finish it. By the time I did mine, I
fully realized the reason for finishing it. I was guided by a
gloved hand. I was allowed to experience recovery and was
not judged on my promptness. I believe that the more you
need to experience it the longer you'll need, and God will
tell you when it needs to be done.

WHAT DIRECTION DO YOU GIVE FOR WRITING THE FOURTH STEP?

CHARLES: If they don't know what their patterns are,
they are going to make the mistakes over and over again.
However, they might be able to recognize their patterns if
they're aware of them as they make these same mistakes.

No, I don't think there should be a time limit. It took
me what it took me. I couldn't read or write when I got
into the program. I'd lost that ability. Therefore, I don't
have a time limit. I think by anywhere around three years
they should've worked a Fourth Step. I definitely think they
should be writing and talking to a sponsor on a regular basis
about it, if they're not. I go by that. If they want to sponsor
somebody, then they should've worked through their Fourth
Step, and all the steps at least once.

JEANETTE: In my first one, I was more concerned about
using proper grammar. My sponsor said "It's nice; it's a
little shallow." That offended me. I try to get across the
idea that this is going to be an ongoing process. I let one
girl do a personal narrative, a stream of consciousness.
Sometimes I suggest they keep it so they can look at it from
time to time, to keep it for the relevance it might have in
their lives. I don't worry about pulling an Eighth Step list

from it. It is not a source of guilt, but of enlightenment. The Fourth Step gives you a new perception of a situation; I tell sponsees to keep it as a checkpoint. Many newcomers feel that they're on God's black list.

M.T.: It's been my experience that sponsees don't know how to tackle the Fourth Step. I've had many questions and more confusion about how to do it from sponsees ready to write, so I give lots of direction. I tell them to get a notebook or pad and number each page at the top with the earliest time they have any memories to the present. Then, on each page, next to their physical age, to put any significant landmarks and any of the following that apply: where they lived at the time (especially if they moved a lot), whatever school grade corresponds to their age from kindergarten up, whatever they have as a signpost for that year that distinguishes it from the ones around it—that keeps it from blending in, i.e. that was the summer we went camping in Oregon or the first year I went to summer camp. Then to proceed to fill in the pages with memories and things that stand out—resentments toward classmates or teachers, fears that they had then, disappointments, relationships with parents and siblings and notes on changes in those relationships, from year to year, when they first did what drugs or drank. By the end, their lives are pretty well laid out, then the unmanageability and where many neurosis started are clearly visible. I devised this for myself. I'd had so many relationships I couldn't remember when they all took place or where I was at with them. The only thing that stood out were the resentments. I had resentments towards my mother and others, and I knew if I wanted to be thorough, there'd be no way for me to remember if I pulled them willy nilly out of a hat as they came to me. When I started to put this chronology together, I found out what I was up to—the drugs, everything, just as it happened. It was amazing. I could feel what I felt then as I wrote down my fourteenth year. The

reason for the grade levels and other distinguishing landmarks is because of the way I filed things: some were filed
by grade and not by age, others by summer vacations, others
by what relationship I was in. To get a comprehensive, thorough Fourth Step, I wanted to get everything relevant. Anything they "filed" by any topic is fine to use.

When they're done with the chronology, I have them list
on separate sheets (sometimes we do this during the Fifth
Step itself) resentments, fears, character defects, etc., which
we go over and ultimately get an amends list from and the
work for the Sixth and Seventh Steps.

BEA: I talk it over with them. First, I find out if they're
writers, if they enjoy writing. Someone who enjoys writing
is more creative, and I would just let them write an auto-
biography, which is what I did. I just started from my childhood and worked my way to the present. I broke it down
into chapters, from childhood to twelve, from thirteen to
nineteen, etc. But, I also have a Fourth Step questionnaire
I've put together from the recovery house that I was in,
from the different texts; I pulled a few questions from everything and made a little format that I think covers what needs
to be dealt with. So, I'll give them that. I just stress for
them to write anything that comes up, whether it's good,
bad, or indifferent. If it comes up and has some kind of
impression on you, just write it down, get it out.

LISA: It depends upon the person. Sometimes I have
sponsees write it autobiographically, sometimes in sections,
and sometimes with one of the little helpful booklets from
the program. But usually I don't recommend those, unless
somebody really needs a lot of direction. I like it to be
autobiographical.

KAREN: I work the Fourth Step in columns, just like the
Big Book says. I have them write all resentments first, then

go back up and explain why and what it affects in them, etc. If they have a resentment that is so big (e.g., molested by their father), I have them just write out in longhand, page after page, just on that, before I ask them to write anything in columns.

NATALIE: When they're ready to write it, I tell them to list their liabilities and assets. I tell them if they don't remember, not to tax themselves. It's simple, but there will be lots of cobwebs at the beginning. It's not a book of fear. It's a book of life. It's a lifesaving kit. If you keep it simple and don't make it hard, it becomes easy.

PATRICE: Read the NA text or the *Big Book*, the *Twelve and Twelve*, then use a guide or the book method, but do it! That's the most important part of this step, doing it.

ED: Just to do it. What we're doing is trying to find out how we react to things, without judging ourselves—what we do when things happen to us, just looking at it and trying to be as honest as possible. That's the big thing, being honest with yourself, admitting this is how things were, this is how things are, and accepting, without judgement.

SUZANNE: I give people a choice. There are a series of questions, numerous questions, that have been created by Hazelden and some of the companies that do a lot of program work. I'll also give them the option to do the columns from the *Big Book*. For me, I don't really think it makes any difference, whatever way people can do it and feel more comfortable with in the beginning. Then, over time, I think most people get down to just using the simplified column version in the *Big Book*. But sometimes when people are newly sober, it's just so simple, it evades them. They can't do it. So, I let people make the choice.

MARIASHA: I don't have it memorized. I have a guide that I wrote that I give to my sponsees, and I suggest they look at that. When I did my inventory, I pretty much followed the old, basic form. I made a list of my resentments; I made a list of my fears. I did my inventory before we had a Fourth Step guide. To be honest with you, the Fourth Step guide scared me, because I'm a perpetual student. There are so many questions. In my mind, each one of those questions could be ten, twenty pages. There's such redundancy; they all cover much of the same material. It's not complicated, it's just so cumbersome. I know people swear by it and think it's great, but I liked just the clean list of resentments and who I was angry at, what my fears were. I didn't do an autobiographical version. I was able to make a list; it was very manageable. I'd work on six or three, or however many I felt I could handle at a sitting. I had a beginning and an end. I tend to have my sponsees follow that format, because it worked for me. But if one of my sponsees said, "I've got the Fourth Step guide, and I'd like to use it." I would say, "Great. Call me if you have any questions, and we'll go through them together."

CHARLES: I do three versions. I do the book version, the four columns, actually it's five columns the way I write it out. I do the Clancy West City Group version, which is seven questions. Then I also have my own Fourth Step that I like to do, which is a little more extensive. It gets a little bit more of their background, dealing mostly with their first years of making choices, from the ages of five to sixteen. I have them list all the people they knew between five and sixteen. Then we go down the list and see what the relationships were with these people. And we get into it. Actually, that's how you do a good First Step: you see what those relationships were, and it falls right into the Fourth Step. It works right through the Second and Third, and into the Fourth.

LEIGH: I wrote down people's names and how I felt about them. I think it's dangerous to masturbate our victimization in a moral inventory. I like columns. I trust my sponsor to get the fruits of my work.

DANNY: I let them know that it's not suppose to be their life story or the great novel. It's a means of getting in touch with those dark places in our lives, and it's also a way of getting in touch with the good places in our lives.

MARGE: The first thing I tell people is they need to be aware of how they're feeling when they're writing it. If they get in emotional difficulty, simply to stop and call or whatever, not to press it. There's no point in getting into so much emotional pain that you want off the planet. The other thing is, I want them to be in a safe place physically. A lot of times they come to my house because they feel safe there. I think it's real important to neutralize as many surroundings as you can, so you can really let it come out.

If sponsees have a particular format they want to use, I have no problem with that, though I usually look at it first. If not, I have some formats that helped me. For example, to take character defects out of the realm of intellect and put them in reality. I don't have any set pattern, I think everybody needs to approach that from their own perspective. I always make sure they get to a certain point with their Fourth Step. That point is, I think, to determine what the fears are underneath the actions of the character defects. Those fears are what need to be removed. Otherwise, when the fear is activated, the character defects will continue. So in one way or another, whether it's before, during, or after the Fifth Step, I try to make sure that that's accomplished.

As part of Step Four, I have people identify the character defect and the fear connected with each instance where they were disappointed in themselves or did whatever. The fear, which is underneath the character defect, is what needs to be removed, otherwise the cause is still there.

WHAT IS YOUR PART, AS A SPONSOR, IN DOING A FIFTH STEP?

BOB B.: There are probably many ways of doing it, because people have different experiences. Some people like to go to what I call a spiritual center: by the ocean, in the woods, up a tree, in the field, on the ground, whatever the case may be. Whatever works, works. I think it's just a matter of being quiet, to have undivided attention. It becomes important for the person that is giving the attention to be attentive, interested in what's going on or has transpired, and, at some point, to give some feedback in terms of his own experience about those particular areas that are sensitive, or if he had any experiences. Sometimes it's just a matter of being heard. Sometimes there is no response required other than the person doing it. Very often, I think it's the sponsor's responsibility to hear and to be able to hear with another ear, in terms of whether it's just story time: Is he telling me what I want to hear or is he talking from somewhere down inside? Is it just a story; is it just a novel; is it a glorified drama? Is its importance underscored? Sometimes we have to look at it in that sense in order to be helpful to that other individual. We need to be able to hear those types of things and to address them in order to be affected by another person.

LEIGH: It's an honor to receive a Fifth Step. My responsibility is to listen and to share my experience, strength and hope and receive the moments of intimacy. Share and respond, make them feel like they're not the strangest person around. Share your stories so they don't feel like the Lone Ranger. Break the moment of isolation. Have a pad and write out character defects and shortcomings. Check off the defect and the appropriate fear.

NATALIE: When hearing a Fifth Step, listen and don't judge. I don't give advice unless I'm asked. When it's done, take a match and burn it. Then it's gone, and you get on with your life. It's a cleansing.

BEA: To listen. To really listen. To take notes. To write down. I wrote down patterns of when I saw character defects come up. Just a little note, and then go back over it. I try to let them read the whole thing before I tell my little stories, my little anecdotes, and my similarities and circumstances. I just want them to feel loved, to feel very comfortable. It's not a big deal. My sponsor, she'd just kick back with a pen and write. I thought, "She's not even listening to me. She could be writing her diary for all I know." But she took notes, then went over them with me. It was real pertinent, sharp things that caught my attention.

DANNY: This was something that I learned from another sponsor. Part of reading or hearing a Fifth Step is digging a little deeper sometimes and asking some more questions to a particular response, helping the sponsee to see the character defects, when the patterns are represented, sometimes asking how he feels about a certain thing now. There was the Fifth Step that a guy read me. He felt he had something to do with his twin brother dying in an accident. He broke down and started crying. This was one of the big things that spun him out and really accelerated his disease. It might have been good for him to sit down with a therapist, even for a couple of sessions to talk about it, but just from the knowledge that I have and the experience with dealing with death, we were able to get to the point where he realized this has happened and no amount of drugs or tears will bring his brother back, and the thing to do now is to go on and do positive things in his memory. It was one of those things that he just briefly touched on. And it was only when I started asking more questions about it, that the whole thing really came out.

....

So, I think the sponsor's role in the Fifth Step also is to let a sponsee know that he's not the only one that did the things that are talked about in the Fourth and Fifth Steps. I think it's really important for him in terms of his own validation as being okay that he knows that some of those dark secrets, or whatever they are, weren't just his. We feel like we're the worst, and that's one of the things that drive people nuts about doing the Fourth Step, feeling like nobody else has done this. I let this one fellow know that there's nothing that he could put in his Fourth Step that would surprise me. The bottom line is we're taking an inventory of basically what our life was about and seeing it's not like that anymore. I think it's important to show the fact that in the course of all these negatives and liabilities that were listed and talked about, a lot of them have already been reversed and are now assets. Sponsees have something to be grateful for and keep a focus on.

MARGE: I think there are several responsibilities that make my "wish list." The first thing I want is neutrality, to be nonjudgmental and have an atmosphere of love and openness. To get that, I pray a lot. The second thing I want is awareness, so that I'm able to be a channel, to point out patterns and those kinds of things. Also, to be attentive. I find it horrifying that some sponsors fall asleep when their babies (sponsees) are sharing their Fifth Step. I would find it unconscionable to ignore someone like that during a process that I consider to be extremely important. Trust is the big issue in Fifth Step work, and that was not something that I had experienced a lot of. The trust for me came from the absolute feeling of neutrality my sponsor had when she did my Fifth Step with me. So, to me, that is something I want to establish and pass on. The only way I know I can get to that is by allowing God to help. So, prayer and meditation would be the way I prepare for a Fifth Step. I would suggest preparation of that mood of meditation and peace. If a sponsee did not get to any of her character defects, it would be fine if she got the trust, because there is time to get to whatever it is if there is the trust. I think it's impossible to do a thorough and fearless moral inventory your first time. I don't know of anybody's that wasn't fearful and incomplete. I don't think that's a requirement. But I think I would rather have the fear reduced than the thorough taken care of, only because it was the safety I have had with the people that have sponsored me that allowed me to be able to write or talk about whatever was going on with me: the pain, issues, things that I've done that I'm ashamed of, etc. It took me years to get some of those things out of my mouth. It took me years to realize that I needed to say some of those things. But because I had that bond, and that safety, when most things came up, I was able to participate in that.

The most important responsibility is availability. I had a personal experience where I had completed my Fourth Step to the best of my ability and my sponsor kept putting off my Fifth Step. It's like a bird that wants to fly while someone holds it in the nest. So I try, as best I can, to accommodate my sponsees when they're finished with their Fourth Step or anticipate being finished. Another thing I try to get across is the purpose of a Fifth Step: to get rid of whatever we can that's in the way of loving on the level we're on, to move on and to continue to do that. It's not a blame thing. It's a discarding and a discovering thing. As it's said in the program: uncover, discover, discard. I think the purpose of any kind of self-examination and release is simply to get rid of what's in our original state. After, what we end up with is the love.

LISA: Listen without judging. Share my own experience, if I have something close to what they're sharing, especially if it's difficult for them, and write down assets and defects as we're going along.

MARIASHA: If one of my sponsees was hearing somebody else's Fifth Step, I think I would ask my sponsee to ask her sponsee if she had any expectations or requests. For example, there are some people who don't want to be interrupted, they want to be able to go straight through. I would just encourage my sponsee to be sensitive and to try, as best she could, or without comprising her own integrity, to meet the needs of that kind of therapy. I don't feel like sponsors have to place a tremendous burden on themselves to analyze what they're hearing. It's important to self-disclose and to convey a sense of compassion when they're listening. If there are any rituals that work for them that they want to pass on, that's fine. Everybody has his or her own thing. I would say give any specific direction, make any suggestions, and come from that place of knowing what it feels like to be vulnerable in front of another human being and to reveal your deepest, darkest feelings to somebody else.

LOIS: When I hear a Fifth Step, I don't give value judgements. The main thing I do is look for patterns in what I'm hearing, so I can point them out after. In the patterns, we often discover what we particularly have to work on when it comes to the Sixth and Seventh Steps.

ED: Listen. Share some of your experiences. Don't judge. Set aside enough time so that you can give the sponsee 100% of your attention, like one long meditation. Set aside a quiet place, where you won't be interrupted. Don't answer the phone. Even better, turn it off. If the sponsee prays, begin and end with a prayer. If not, begin and end with a moment of silence.

This is a very special time. Someone is learning to trust you. Be there.

PATRICE: Don't do a Fifth Step with anyone until you've worked your own Fourth and Fifth Steps. This is a program of experience being shared. That's why it works so well. It's success building on success.

JEANETTE: On the Fifth Step, try to have something positive come out of it, regardless of how negative it is. If there are things revealed that are extremely damaging in nature, always suggest a therapist: There is only so much a sponsor can do. Some of the deepest problems can not be handled by a sponsor/sponsee relationship. You don't say, "Oh, I can't handle this," but "Have you thought about getting some help with this?"

KAREN: Hopefully, if everything has gone as planned, most of the big things my sponsee has in her Fourth Step are things we've already talked about, and hopefully we've shared enough about ourselves to each other that she is comfortable telling me anything and everything. I will also share similar things about myself as we do her Fifth Step so she won't feel like it's all about her alone. I listen and share throughout the whole Fifth Step.

M.T.: This is an important question. It's been my experience that what I do during the Fifth Step determines what kind of experience my sponsees have with that step. I have found that even though they may have written as searching an inventory as they could and been as thorough as they could in putting down the facts, but without my help in interpreting the information, they would have left with a lot less insight than they did.

It is of the utmost importance, when a sponsee allows herself to be vulnerable by bringing me her flaws, secrets, pains, resentments and embarrassments, that I don't further diminish her self-esteem, cast blame, ridicule or in any way invalidate experiences that were emotionally charged for her. I think it's key to maintain this understanding, the significance of the Fourth Step contents (even if they don't seem that dramatic to me), and be sensitive to my sponsees pain and vulnerability.

On the other hand, it's key to find the patterns of behavior at work, to be able to interpret what we hear, give guidance and help clear up things that are confusing or that she has been using to beat herself up with.

When we get together to do it, I make sure I have the day free, and we're alone and won't be disturbed for many hours. My own Fifth Step took all day (with lunch and snack breaks), but those I've heard have taken about two to four hours. I take notes and suggest they just start reading. I'll ask questions if I'm confused about something. The process has been amazing when I focused and really listened and then have a perception about something read. It's key to participate fully, to hear, and to be willing to explore. We were halfway through a sponsee's Fifth Step, when she went over her fifteenth year (as I've said, I have them do a chronology of their lives). She casually mentioned her first boyfriend and went on to the next item, as if there wasn't anything significant about that relationship. Knowing how loaded relationships usually are, I stopped her and asked for some details. She gave some basic facts: his age, name, how long they went out, etc. Talking about it didn't seem to bring up anything special either. But I had a feeling there was more. I had to ask a series of questions before it came out that he had beaten her violently for the length of their relationship, that she had really gotten into doing drugs with him, and that he did tremendous damage to her not just physically, but emotionally as well! Why hadn't she told me? Before that point, she wasn't in touch with any anger toward him. In fact, the relationship she focused on and felt worse about was with another guy many years later (which

was nowhere near as dysfunctional), never seeing that vio-
lence, though mild compared to the first guy, was a pattern
in her life that stemmed back to her childhood. She had no
criteria to judge by before that. She got the most freedom
from these hidden demons that had been keeping her self-
worth at a minimum because of my willingness to delve,
assume more than meets the eye (remember: our disease
wants to keep us in the dark), and ask probing questions. I
make them keep their Fourth Step so they can use it for
their Eighth Step list. A boyfriend suggested I burn my resentments section, and I did, and I was very unhappy about
that when I realized *my* part in those resentments, and
couldn't remember all the people listed who, by the time I
got to the Eighth Step, deserved my amends!

SUZANNE: Listen, be very supportive, and share with
that person one or two of your secrets you had when you
did your Fourth Step with your sponsor. That way they
don't feel like they're alone in sharing their incomprehen-
sible, demoralizing behaviors with you. It's like, ''Oh yeah,
I know about those behaviors. I've had them myself.'' Also,
I always take the Fourth Step and burn it.

CHARLES: A lot of us drive our sponsees around in the
car, and make them tell us, or read us, the Fourth Step in
the car while we're driving someplace. By the time they get
through telling us, we stop and eat. Then we go back home
and have a moment where they can be alone, to see if there's
anything else that comes up for them. That is the pattern
which we've fallen into. I didn't do my Fifth Step in a car.
But I think that's a good place to do it. So I would suggest
that to people; I think it works out fine that way. There's
something soothing about riding around. There's something
good about that. Driving your sponsee around gives you
something to do while he's reading.

Chapter Six

Steps Six and Seven

"I spend a lot of time going over what
a character defect is, what an asset
is, when a defect becomes an asset,
and vice versa."

— PATRICE

What direction can you give in working Steps Six and Seven?

Steps Six and Seven, where we are ready to have our character defects removed and humbly ask God to do so, are internal processes. But we count on our sponsor's direction on all of the steps. What can you, as a sponsor, offer as guidance on these important and often quickly passed over steps?

M.T.: The work of the Sixth and Seventh Steps, I believe, is to be constantly willing to realize what we are acting on and see how that gets in the way of our spiritual development, that character defects are the things barring the door to the spirit. The fact is, we are not all murderers, so our defects are not extremely obvious things we are in a rush to get rid of because society is down on us to do so. Most of the stuff my sponsees and I have worked on is mild, but important, and detrimental to their growth. As long as we are willing to ignore them, they don't go away. Nothing goes away that we aren't willing to release. Along with Steps One and Three, I think Steps Six and Seven are the most important steps to be worked. I stress them strongly and expect my sponsees to work them thoroughly and actively, like they did their Fourth. It's been my experience that the awakening from these steps is profound and easily missed if they are lightly examined, as they so often are because people cop out, thinking God's doing all the work.

KAREN: From the Fifth step, we pull out a list of character defects. For the Sixth and Seventh Steps I have my sponsee recognize, embrace, and own those defects. Then, I have her pray that they be removed and also come up with ways for her to do things differently, so she is no longer practicing those defects. For instance, if we've come up with jealousy as a defect, I might tell her whenever she feels it creeping up (someone got a promotion at work, someone's getting married, etc.), before any feelings of anger or resentment can fester, go right up to that person and warmly congratulate her and tell her how happy she is for her. Keep doing this and eventually you will mean it and pretty soon you will no longer possess that character defect. At the same time, pray for the ability to do this and for the defect to be removed.

MARIASHA: We just work on becoming willing. We work on prayer and surrender, going back to the first three steps, getting back to that place where you're willing to let go, willing to pay attention when you're acting on your shortcomings, and willing to let them go.

JEANETTE: The Sixth Step is an attitude that is supposed to have evolved by the time you get to this step. If a sponsee says, "I feel I'm not ready," I tell her to go back to Steps Four and Five until she is ready to divest. It's an attitude that develops. Sometimes, if a sponsee say she is not ready, I let it go until she is ready.

PATRICE: This step is one that can bring up a lot of shame for people because it's about who they are at the core, not that they do bad things. I spend a lot of time going over what a character defect is, what an asset is, when a defect becomes an asset and vice versa. I cover all the ways these have helped people to survive, and how, at some point, they started destroying instead of helping. Survival tools gone wrong, but with a little work, they can be useful again.

SUZANNE: I always ask them to write down their list of character defects and always suggest that, in addition to writing down the ones they think they have, they ask people who are close to them, like their parents, siblings, or a partner, what they think. Additionally, I ask that they listen to these people and write down what's being said, so they can cross-reference their own list with the others.

ED: These steps are about accepting "being human." Relax. You are powerless over your defects. All you can do is be aware of them. When they pop up, say to yourself, "Isn't that interesting? I'm so angry." Talk to your defect as if it were an old friend. "Oh, you knucklehead, what are you up to now?"

LEIGH: As you're going through the fears and character defects, say, "What is the pattern?" It becomes crystal clear if you're praying. You do these steps for the rest of your life.

BEA: Step Six we'll write out. Sometimes we'll take it from an inventory. I like to get rid of the inventory. I got rid of mine. I think it's good to burn it. Burn it and it's gone. I also have a list of character defects, we'll sit down and go through them. I'll ask her, "Do you think this applies to you?" If she says no, I'll say, "Think again. You know, what about . . ." I'll bring up a circumstance or something. She'll have her list, and I want her to pray on it. Just take time and pray on it, be willing to let God change them. The more you pray on it, the more you notice them changing.

MARGE: First of all, I think that the most important thing is to get to underlying fear that triggers the character defect. Sometimes that's very specific. However, there are only so many fears people can have. As it was explained to me in Step One, I could either pray for the obsession to drink to be removed, or I could give it away, therefore experiencing a whole new deal. I do Six and Seven the same way—coming to a willingness to place my fears in God's hands, in order to be relieved of those triggers. People talk about pushing the buttons. Tris, my mentor, always used to say, "The trick is get rid of the buttons." Giving those fears, those buttons, to God is the most important thing you can do. I believe that when we actually are willing and we give those fears on the level that we're experiencing them to God, we're placed in a context where, in the same repetitive experience, we cannot go back and get the same fears. I've heard other people share this and several weeks later found out that they've walked through the very same situation, but their perception was totally different. It either was not perceived as a problem, as anything to resist, or was handled in another way with an ease they had never experienced before. That's how I gauge, and tell my people to gauge, whether they have done Six and Seven sincerely or not. Simply not to make a big deal out of it, but if they experience the same thing on the same level again, they know they were unwillingly to release it on the level they are on. And I keep saying "on the level they're on" because it's been my experience that character defects don't come back on the same level that you've given them away on, but there are different levels of those character defects. The operation and recognition become more subtle as we go on, after getting rid of the big chunks. I recommend sponsees put those things in an imaginary bundle in their hands and release them to God. That's what I did with my drinking, and it worked. So, that's the way I do Six and Seven. There is an absolute joy that comes out of doing something willingly, rather than out of a fear of not doing it. And, giving it away, rather than having it removed, is the highest experience. It's like praying praises instead of anything else. It's a totally joyful, rather than a punitive, type of release. I encourage that in every step.

BOB B.: I think the big thing is the decision, because some people get the understanding that they have some power other than God's power, especially when talking about correcting their character defects. I look at character defects as part of our very brain, developed ever since we started developing character. In a lot of the instances, we don't see them because they have become such an integral part of our lives. It is very difficult for us to tell whether that's an outside thing or an inside thing. As far as character defects being internal things, I think we don't completely know their total impact or understand much about them. So, we have to learn how to be willing to give up those parts of our character, even parts we think give us a certain amount of pleasure, that are not serving us well. I can't remove those if you asked me to remove them. We need to become knowledgeable about these defects; they are something to become aware of, something we have to work at, something we just have to keep in the forefront. We need to make a list and take some action on these defects and correct them as often as possible. Are we going to do it everyday? Take a checklist every time you go out the door. Stop being late. Stop doing this here. Be more attentive to that. Take care of that and don't just pass on it, you need to be doing something about it. Start altering what you do about it. I try to keep those kind of instances separate from, yet still part of, the same character problems that I need to deal with.

Chapter Seven

The Amends Steps

"I feel that the secret of amends is,
'I know I've hurt you. What do you
want me to do to make it right?'"

— DON

"There is nothing
you have to face alone."

— BOB B.

Some suggestions for working the amends steps.
What to suggest to a sponsee with outstanding
legal problems.

....

There are as many ways to handle amends as there are people who need to make them. Trying to figure out what the correct amends are for someone else to make, we all know, can be tricky. (It's hard enough to work on your own.) And, what if there are legal issues, which many addicts and alcoholics face coming into recovery? Here again, you have the benefit of many years experience on these important steps and some ideas you can adapt for situations that may arise for you.

....

SOME SUGGESTIONS FOR WORKING THE AMENDS STEPS.

....

JEANETTE: It can take time to be ready to make an Eighth Step list. I tell them nothing is black or white, just put down your part. Making direct amends is tricky. You cannot make amends to people who have died. If it's possible, go to the grave and talk to them. If it's not possible, write a letter and burn it or do what you want with it. Once they've committed how they feel to paper, they can see it. This is very important because you can deny what you've said and thought, but, in black and white, on paper, you cannot deny it. One sponsee wrote a letter and burned it and mixed the ashes with her father's ashes. The Ninth Step is all about willingness. One woman's husband stole from many people. He broke into houses in the '50s and stole

TVs. It would have been a horrendous volume of calls, harmful to him and to the people he was calling if he tried to make direct amends. But he was willing to make amends, and he acknowledged his wrongs.

KAREN: I believe in making direct amends whenever possible. When it isn't possible, I come up with creative ways of making amends, often with the input of my sponsee. This could be something like writing a letter that will never be sent in the case of a deceased person or finding someone else (like a sick person) who could use a visitor and doing this in the name of the person who is no longer here.

I always tell my sponsees to stay out of relationships, at least for the first year, if they're not currently in one, and then we'll talk. I also try to have them work the steps at least the first nine steps during the first year, then they can continue to make their amends, pray, and mediate and be of service after that.

M.T.: As far as I'm concerned, the most important thing is becoming willing—really willing. One of my sponsors once said, "You need to get to neutral before you make an amend," and I agree. I got to see this first hand with an amend I wanted to make. I owed money for a piece of art and I hadn't completed making the payments because I was supporting my addiction. When I got to that amend, I was ready to pay the balance with cash. The painting had increased in value during the time that had elapsed. But I wasn't willing to give the art back, *even if that was what the person wanted*. I had done a wrong, but I was only willing to right it as I saw fit, not as it may have needed to be done. The point was, I wasn't really willing to make the amend, to make it right. But the point of an amend, as I understand it now, is to make it right for the person who was wronged, to the best of our ability, and in doing so, making it right for ourselves. I got to the right place with it and that realization came with it. It was the pivotal issue, and I still think, one of the most important.

PATRICE: Never work this step without first discussing it with a sponsor and, if at all possible, don't work this step out of order, because I've seen a lot of people harmed, both the recovering people and the people they were making amends with. This is a very important step and can turn lives around if used/worked correctly.

SUZANNE: It's very important to make amends, except when to do so would harm yourself or others. A lot of times people have issues with the government, with the law, with the person they're married to. I find it isn't appropriate to go back and start digging things up again. I also find a lot of times people want to beat themselves up, let go, and tell their partner, "Oh, I had fifteen affairs, and I've slept with your boss. And I did this, and I did that." At this point in time, the marriage is really good, so declaring that is not appropriate. So I have people go over it with me first: who they're going to do it with and why, to help them determine what's appropriate and what's not. I think a lot of times people aren't really clear about that when they're newly sober. It's not appropriate to call up the I.R.S. and turn yourself in if you have three children and can't afford to make those financial amends and, as a result, put your whole family in jeopardy.

LEIGH: On the Eighth Step list, I see if they really need to make amends to them. Because of our guilt, we think we need to make amends. God provides. My sponsor told me I'd be adding and taking off names for the rest of my life. Most importantly is owning responsibility and changing behavior.

ED: My sponsor didn't really give me any suggestions, just do your best to change. That's what an amend is, a change.

NATALIE: My sponsees didn't make direct amends. It would have injured themselves or others. I think what we think of ourselves is really important. I'll ask what someone else thinks, if I want to know. As long as I'm doing something with a right motive, that's what counts. Also, am I willing to change? I tell them to think about the situation if it were reversed: how would they want that person to come to them? Faith and fear do not live in the same body. What I fear most I write on paper and put in the "God can." I give it to God to handle, then I do what's put in front of me. The results are already in. Whatever happens is supposed to happen.

MARGE: My sponsor didn't give me any direction about amends. But, my amends were not to specific people. I pretty well hated the world. My amends were to be a totally different person, to get rid of the fear that caused me to put people down and do those kinds of things I did before I got sober.

The Ninth Step in the *Big Book* says something very interesting. It says we're not after saying "I'm sorry." We're after the spiritual experience, and it's a marvelous, difficult, but involved one. I don't think it should be rushed. I think there's more inside to be gained from your Eighth and Ninth Steps and the process of that than probably anything else, when you first start to do them.

MARIASHA: My sponsor never gave me any direction about making amends. She just listened to what I had done, what I wanted to do, what I thought would be best.

There have been a few amends that my sponsees have needed to make that were not appropriate to be made directly. What we've done is try to examine ways that amends could be made where their safety and well being would not be jeopardized. I think you just have to get creative.

My husband has an interesting story. As a teenager he stole plants from a nursery and gave them to all his friends. He decided that he was going to make an amends when he got clean. So, he went to the nursery and asked to speak with the person in charge. The manager asked my husband how much he thought he stole. My husband figured about $200. The manager took him into the back room, rang up $200 on the cash register and added the sales tax. He paid it in full, but it was a humbling experience of taking full responsibility for what he had done.

The most powerful of the amends I made was to an aunt and uncle from whom I had taken a little money. I sent them money, along with a letter where I told them, "Please, whatever you do, don't send this money back to me. If you choose not to keep it, that's fine, but I'm seeking your understanding and support for what I need to do in order to take responsibility for what I've done." They wrote back, telling me how proud they were, that they understood I was in pain and were happy to see that I had found recovery, and out of respect for my wishes, they were going to keep the money. They kept my money, allowing me to take responsibility for what I'd done, and honored that I needed to do that. They didn't need my money. They didn't keep it because they needed to be reimbursed; it was something that had happened many years before. But they understood that was what I needed to do. That was very comforting for me. I grew a lot as a result of that.

CHARLES: I was making amends way before I got sober. I was in such pain. So, my sponsor gave me some direction. He asked, "Do you have to dig that up again? Is that amends really necessary?" He's also helped me with people who have died or with people I couldn't find. He said, "Why don't you just make amends to somebody else? Give it to somebody else." I think the hardest amends for me to make were the financial amends. I could make all the verbal amends I wanted to. I could get through those, but the amends where it actually takes cash out of your pocket and puts it into somebody else's is the most difficult and the easiest to cheat on, although you're really just cheating your-self.

With amends, they don't have to be direct. Amends can be indirect; they can be something you do for somebody else, but you really need to make sure that's what it really is, that it's not just trying to get out of making amends.

BOB B.: Amends of different kinds: amends that we don't make, that we need to make, that we're still in the process of making. I think it's something you have to finish, that you have to do. Very often you're talking about amends that could cause you grievous harm, amends that could cause you irreparable damage in terms of a disruption in your life or somebody else's. There are probably people who you have lost contact with or who have passed away that you have some unfinished business with. In this case, I have in-structed sponsees to write a letter and mail it or to go visit the grave site and leave the message, to say all the things they want to say, but write them out. Or they can get the number, call the person and tell them about what they're trying to do and so forth.

You get all kinds of responses. In most cases, I've found most people want good will. But there are instances where it might irreparably hurt the relationships that are still going on. You don't want to go back and tell someone, "Hey, I slept with your old lady. We ran off to the Bahamas. That's where we were when we were gone that week." You don't want to do that. Whether they may have known it or not.

I try to encourage people to take care of amends, and let them know they can write it now. Don't wait, because we don't know if we can meet them tomorrow. And the more you get out of the way the less you have to do. Better get as much of that out of the way as you can.

Willingness is one of the big things we have to keep open to. Regardless of what we think about it, if we got it on our list of amends, evidently it must be something we need to straighten out. That would be about the business of doing it, of taking action. Action is part of the magic, whether it's writing, sending money anonymously (Give cash to some agency, person, or place anonymously with a little explanation like "Sorry about the transgression of . . . This is what you have coming. I hope you forgive me for whatever I've done. I'm sorry I can't put a name, address, or place on it, but it doesn't make any difference.") or making amends with someone who has died. Write a message saying, "This is what I would intend to happen, that you would forgive me for what transpired. I'm sorry I didn't take care of this while you here," and carry the message to that grave site and leave it.

WHAT TO SUGGEST TO A SPONSEE WITH OUTSTANDING LEGAL PROBLEMS.

ED: Get a lawyer.

CHARLES: Take care of them. Show up. I've found, people are just scared to death of their tickets. I've never had a sponsee who went to jail for admitting what was wrong or going to the authorities with what he thought was going to put him in jail. I haven't had a sponsee that killed or murdered anybody. I still have sponsees who haven't taken care of their drunken driving. I sponsor them on it all the time. I encourage them to go and take care of it, before they go to jail.

If necessary, I tell them to talk to a professional. I have people in the program I would suggest that they consult, who usually do that for free, until it gets to court. I have known people who have done jail time in their first year who are still sober today. But in most instances it doesn't seem to be valuable to walk into AA, walk out the door, walk up to a judge, give yourself up, and spend the next six years in jail. The quality of AA in Santa Monica is a lot better than the quality in San Quentin.

BEA: I was told to surrender. I had to turn myself in. If I was going to start living a clean and sober life, this is what I had to do. If the issue comes up, I recommend to people I sponsor, whether somebody is chasing them for money or there's another problem, that they do the right thing. That's what we're learning how to do. But I don't *demand* they do the right thing. I don't demand, because I don't know if it's really my business. I'm not God; I don't know, but I feel the right thing to do is to be honest.

LEIGH: See a lawyer. Deal with this stuff, don't avoid it. This is really about change and living with ourselves. Do service and work with people. I believe they must physically do something. Take the time. Give to charity, but they must pay back what they've taken.

NATALIE: Someone with outstanding legal problems must pay eventually. If they're not caught they should amend immediately, change their ways right now.

DANNY: One of my first sponsees came to the program with a legal problem, felony possession and trafficking in another state. He was in the hands of an attorney; that's all we could do. I got another fellow who had a bunch of things he hadn't taken care of, and as a result, he couldn't get a driver's license. I said, "You have to clean this up." It wasn't the same as waiting until he got to his Ninth Step; this is stuff that's now, and he could deal with it. It was simply a matter of, in one case, paying the money. There are certain things that sponsees have to do by the rules; if it's something legal, they just have to go do what it takes.

MARIASHA: I haven't had that situation. When I've had sponsees who have stolen from department stores, I have not suggested they go back to the department stores. Instead, we found indirect ways to make amends, whether it is donating the value of what was stolen; donating merchandise, articles of clothing, or possessions to others who are less fortunate; or making some kind of a monetary contribution to an organization. If my sponsee had outstanding legal problems, I would probably suggest she get legal counseling; I'm not an attorney, and I can't control or give direction about something I'm not knowledgeable about. Then, together we would look at what was said to her, and maybe I could help her make some decisions that were less threatening.

BOB B.: At the earliest convenience, get it squared away. I have had to walk through this with a lot of people. Collect information, get data. Recently, we were dealing with legal problems and just did letter writing; the person was looking to do amends. One of the things about legal problems is that they're not going away by themselves. So, if you want to feel some comfort, want to feel like you're not being watched or watched over, or want to feel freedom, try to dispose of the legal problems at the earliest convenience. Sometimes, we have to get a few days or months clean, in order to get all the legal ramifications ironed out. I think one of the things a sponsor should know about is how the amends step is best served in terms of whether letters are written or contacts made. Walk through this with the person and let him know that he's not alone. There are some things we can do when we find out that the probation counselor and the legal system want to see some action being taken. In that case, recovery is one of the actions which can be taken that is looked at very favorably. I've found most areas of the judicial system to be very favorable to the program. Sentences may be lessened or conditions altered as a result of recovery. I haven't seen any great harm in the process of doing it. I've only seen very positive reaction; sometimes they had to do time in the cell, because they owed the government time, while others got parole or probation. However, they went back clean; they finished their time or whatever they had to do, with a different attitude, or they utilized that time to do something good. When they got out they were able to continue working the program and get on with their lives. So, legal obstacles are not insurmountable. I think it's a case of having to deal with it and knowing that you're not alone. And I think it is very important you don't have to face it alone. There is nothing you have to face alone.

J.P.: Seek legal advice. Talk to a lawyer. The courts are real sympathetic when you're in recovery. I try to impress upon my sponsees that they need to handle these issues. I was driving an uninsured vehicle when I came in, but people stayed on me about it. I drove my first legal mile when I was fourteen months clean.

LOIS: When my sponsees have serious legal, medical, or psychological problems, I suggest that they go to a professional for help. I think it's a mark of maturity to ask for help when you need it.

SUZANNE: I advise them to face them and get them handled.

PATRICE: I work with them in cleaning up their lives, but I never force them to turn themselves in to the law. They will have to do the time, not me. It's their call. I do support them in seeing the price that they have to pay in not clearing up the past.

JEANETTE: If someone is wanted by the law, they need to make a decision, not you. If it bothers them enough, then something needs to be done. One of the original fifteen Narcotics Anonymous members jumped bail in Texas and was wanted on warrant. He decided to face it, and we all wrote a huge stack of letters on his behalf. The judge was lenient and sentenced him to six months and told him not to come back to Texas. He was originally looking at fifteen years. When it's something that bothers them a lot I tell them, "I will support you in this, in whatever you decide to do. Personally, I believe it needs to be cleaned up." If you say that, you can be seen as a bad guy if it turns out badly—so keep that in mind. You have to look at who is served. So much depends on whether it's going to come down; in that case, the sooner the better. If it's something that is dormant, that's another issue. Many people are stuck with old ideas like, "I'll just hook a little on the side." No. You can't do that, and it isn't necessarily a moral judgement. You must give up the old life style.

SUNNY: I have never had anyone with outstanding legal issues. If I did, I would send them to a proper expert or someone with experience. Part of my job is to know who to send them to. I tell my sponsees to go to a doctor if it's a medical problem. If it were a legal issue, a lawyer, and to take his advice. At least in that way you're properly armed.

Chapter Eight

Addressing Common Issues That May Arise

"It doesn't do me any good for you to tell me I need to get some self-esteem or self-acceptance or I need to turn it over.... It's like telling me I need to speak French.... Teach me, show me through your example how to get to a place of forgiveness."

— MARIASHA

Guidance on resentments, obsession to use, relationships in early recovery, and stealing.

I picked some common issues (resentments, obsession to use,
relationships in early recovery, and stealing) to see if I'd get
some new answers to old questions or if most were practicing
the tried and true suggestions (e.g., no relationships in the
first year, etc.). I got an interesting mix.

GUIDANCE ON RESENTMENTS.

SUNNY: Hit your knees, it works.

JEANETTE: If you have a long, complicated resentment
with a lot of history, write it out and write your part in it.
Try not to write in a one-sided fashion; even if you've been
wrong, you still have to be rid of it. Remember, it's not
for them; it's for you. If it's simple, I suggest you pray,
even unwillingly, wishing for them what you pray for yourself. I suggest prayer about any situation and in time it will
work out okay. You're not hiding anything by hiding your
feelings from God. I prayed for relatives who were trying
to do me in. I prayed against my will. My sponsor said it
wasn't for them, but for me. My stomach was grinding. It
took four years. I wanted revenge. At the end of four years,
I hardly thought of them. It didn't mean we were friends.
I stayed away from them and didn't have them in my home.
But I was free of it. Resentments only hurt us.

SUZANNE: I think resentment is when you take the poison and wait for the other person to die. People have to look at how they can release the resentment, forgive themselves, and the other person and let it go.

ED: For resentments, I point to the Fourth Step guide and to the exercise of finding out what my part was in the resentment. I found, that in each case the resentment was really against myself for being caught, for being exposed as human, for not being something I thought I should be (Superman, God, Jesus Christ, whatever), for being me. Each time, I was at fault. I built up a resentment to defend myself, to keep me from getting too close to the truth. The resentment was a distraction, an attempt to distract myself from myself. The size of the resentment was related to how afraid I was of what I was hiding from myself. So much work and so much time wasted. So, we dig in and find our part and set ourselves free.

CHARLES: What actions can I suggest in resentments? First of all, anything that turns into resentment is naturally something about you, it's not about them. So, you have to go back and see what stopped you, why you have that resentment, see what your part in it was. It has nothing to do with the person you have resentment against. You have to remember that. From there, we write on it together and we would talk about it.

LEIGH: I have a grudge list. "I am resentful to _____ for ____." Resentments are dangerous. I ask my sponsees to share them with me, then do the Sixth and Seventh Steps on them. It doesn't matter how long they have been clean.

NATALIE: To read page 449 in the *Big Book* about acceptance and to write about it. We build expectations and get angry when they don't happen. That anger goes to resentment and then to sickness which will kill us. Communication is very important. Usually, resentments come from lack of communication. We judge the way people do things.

MARGE: I don't believe in resentments. I believe in pain, hurt, and betrayal. I have found for myself that self-righteousness has been my biggest evil. It's what my family functioned on. Therefore, anger is the cheapest thing I can come up with. It's right there all the time. The thing I never want to admit is that I'm hurt or I feel like you've betrayed me in some way. If it's a matter of getting mad at something, I think that anybody needs to be willing to release that. If it goes deeper, I think that needs to be looked at. I felt like my heart had been beaten to death when I got sober, so it took me a long time to admit when I was hurt. I always wanted to be better than that, above it, or not affected by it. So I put it off for a long time. I don't encourage that in my sponsees. I share my unwillingness to deal with my pain and anger for my first several years as an example to show my sponsees they don't have to wait that long.

BOB B.: I think in some instance you need a third party to mediate. There have been of a couple of cases where I knew both of the people involved in the resentment. And I thought both of them are so much alike in both instances. But they're not willing to put themselves in the position of questioning themselves. Their attitude was: this is who I am, this is me; this is the way I think, or this is the way I function, and this is the way I operate; if you don't like it, too bad. Both of them are pretty much the same, of the same temperament and type. I understood why they couldn't talk or communi-

cate. There would have to be a third party to see where
the dividing line is or what's happening between them,
because in the heat of the battle, the two opponents
can't see anything anyhow.

I recommend mediation of a number of sorts, whether
collectively, if you have some people that you work very
closely with who are willing to sit together to look at both
sides and the feelings that go with that and where they come
from. They come from a far off place in terms of the character that we develop through the years. How did we arrive
at that particular type of understanding, feeling, etc. It's
such an integral part of our being that it's not something
that just sorts itself out. It's something that has to be sorted
out. And we can't sort it alone, and we usually can't sort
it out by arguing with one another. There's one person not
willing to listen at some point. To hear the other one out,
there usually has to be somebody standing still between
them to mediate, to see both sides of what's going on. Very
often I say we need someone, whether or not it's a professional. I think sometimes you just need a third party who is
neutral.

You know, writing is almost a daily thing. You need a
journal, a pad, or something that you have when you get
out of the bed with a resentment or go to bed with one
of these nutcrackers on your head. You need to write on
that specific thing whatever it is, because you will see
many things that you didn't see at first. It might change
the whole perspective, your whole perception of what
might be going on, like what you did that ticked someone off. I would write about that one thing, about that
one person, the whys or wherefores, to see what your
feelings are. Then, we'll talk about your feelings and
about what you think the other person's feelings are.
When you write this, it's called inventorying a resentment.

J.P: Resentments in early recovery—put them on hold until your Fourth Step. Put them on the back burner and see whether you still dislike the person by then.

GUIDANCE ON THE OBSESSION TO USE.

SUNNY: Pray for relief of the obsession.

SUZANNE: I think prayer and lots of meetings are the antidote for obsession to use.

ED: For the obsession to use, I tell them to think of something else, to think about what they're going to share at the next meeting or what they'd tell someone else who wanted to use. If they pray, I tell them to pray. The mind can only hold one thought at a time. If they're thinking about not using, then they can't think about using. Sometimes I tell them to repeat the Serenity Prayer again and again, all day long, from the moment they get up to the moment they lay back down to sleep, falling asleep saying the Serenity Prayer.

CHARLES: Obsession to use is a hard one. It's usually because you're not going to meetings, because you're falling out of those meetings, because you're not committed. If I had somebody who was using, I would try to see if he was going to enough meetings and if he was out of doing commitments. Usually, we get ourselves in a place where we mess up on a lot of commitments, then we're unconnected. Then first thing we know, we've got an excuse to go to the medicine cabinet and use. Or we'll use any crisis, like someone's death, to use. I've had good friends (not sponsees) that used over death.

LEIGH: What's it about? Write about it. Share about it. Talk at meetings. What saved my life was to ask God to take it away five minutes at a time. Stay in a meeting. If you're in obsession and not in a meeting, it's very hard to care about the seriousness of this disease. I work for progress, and I can't carry you. You have a choice: take it or not.

BEA: Change the behaviors and I believe the obsession changes along with it. Go to a meeting. Grab a girlfriend. Go pick up a newcomer. Go do something for somebody else and get it out of your head. Come over here; we'll go down to the women's recovery house and see people that are a lot worse off than you are and see if you still want to use.

DON: If drinking thoughts come, don't sit them down and entertain them. Let them pass through. I use to rub my veins because things were tense in my life.

MARGE: If someone is having an obsession to drink and use, she has not given up control to her Higher Power. That's the bottom line. So she has a choice. I usually have her examine very, very closely why she is hanging on to the control of that. Why? What is the payoff? Usually it's because she has not done the grief work of mourning the release of alcohol; then we start on that.

MARIASHA: I try to change the focus; I try to help them gain a deeper understanding of what the dynamic is that's resulting in the obsession. That requires listening to try to understand what is prompting the manifestation, however it may present itself. I don't think things like "Just turn it over," "You have to pray," and "You have to let it go,'' work. It's like saying, "You have to have some self-esteem and self-acceptance." When I heard things like that, my response was, "Great. Now could you please give me the instruction manual on how I do that?" It doesn't do me any good for you to tell me I need to get some self-esteem or self-acceptance or that I need turn it over. Those are foreign concepts to me; it's like telling me I need to speak French. I don't know how to do that. You have to be a little more helpful than that. Teach me, show me through your example, how to get to a place of forgiveness.

What do you do, or what is it that's going on in your life that is causing you to feel so empty, so lonely, or so obsessed? Or why is it you're so resentful? What is it about this person that's troubling you? We try to get to what button that's triggered, because resentment and things of that nature generally have little to do with that particular person. That's more the frosting on the cake; what the resentments trigger is usually a bigger issue. I try to talk with my sponsees and work with them on the bigger issue and try to work the steps on that issue.

BOB B.: I've usually sent them on missions of gratefulness, like go get a newcomer and send or take him down to skid row, take a meeting down on skid row, or go talk to somebody else. Don't be by yourself; get out of where your are and go somewhere where other addicts are recovering. It's the whole dynamic of getting out from where you are. If your head is messing with you, move from that discomfort. Walk down the block; just get away from where you are. Take some action.

J.P.: Frequent meetings and staying with people who don't use. Those who make meetings regularly stay clean.

GUIDANCE ON RELATIONSHIPS IN EARLY RECOVERY.

M.T.: I started one at eleven days clean with someone with one-and-a-half years, but I kept my program up front. It's not something I'd recommend. The ups and downs were stressful, and I could've done without that. I'd get up out of bed to go to a meeting with him saying, "What do you mean you're leaving?" He was always second to my program. I think if that's the case, it's okay. More recently, a relationship almost took me out. We split up, at my request, because I knew there was drink in his future. He no longer went to meetings, wasn't working a program. So I told him we were at a crossroads—I wanted to work a program, and he was picking on me for making so many meetings. So, I wanted out. Several months after we split up, he ended up in detox (again). I would have been with him if I'd stayed in that marriage. Instead, I celebrated nine years clean and sober. It's hard to split up a marriage, but my recovery had to come first. His lack of program had helped bring down the relationship anyway.

I've learned a lot. I can't be with someone who isn't working a program.

SUZANNE: It's suggested that people don't get involved in a relationship in the first year of their recovery. However, I tell people they can do it, but they need to have a lot of support around them, because all of their issues that will show up as a result of it. I'll tell them it will put them in greater jeopardy to use, because it will be very emotional for them. But as long as they're aware of that and they're willing to accept the consequences of it and to commit to not drinking or using no matter what, they'll grow very rapidly and quickly if they're in a relationship.

ED: For relationships, I ask them to tell me, honestly, which they would rather do: go to a meeting or stay home and get laid. They all want to stay home and get laid. The decision is up to them. I tell them to give themselves a year to get to know themselves, to get comfortable with themselves. If they get in a relationship, the temptation is there to think that the other person will make them feel good about themselves, because, in the beginning, she does. When we fall in love, we are really falling in love with ourselves, with the way we are around this person, with who we think we are. All our dreams seem real. We put this tremendous burden on the other person to make us feel good about ourselves, and this becomes her job. Then we get ticked off when she's not doing her job! Sometimes I don't say anything, I just ask them to think about it.

CHARLES: I never had a relationship in early recovery; I stayed single the first year. I dated, and I did not get back into the relationship that I had before I got sober. I stayed away from the person I had dated. I did not live with the person for the whole year. But the minute that year was up, I moved in. That's my experience.

NATALIE: Do not make any major changes in the first year. And do an inventory first.

BEA: They say no relationships. But, I was in a relationship with a newcomer. I believe it is fine as long as you don't make that person your Higher Power. You have to work at that. I suggest women don't get involved. If they get involved, I don't stop sponsoring them. I don't tell them they have to leave the man. I just tell them they have to focus on themselves and work their program, and the relationship will work itself. What they need to do is take care of themselves; that's it.

SUNNY: I suggest no major changes in the first year. No divorce unless you're being beaten. No new relationships, though they'll do it anyway. Tom W. and Larry K. have good tapes on this subject. They say it all. The sponsee needs to look at the short-term gain vs. the long-term gain. I will not mediate a relationship. I ask, "What price are you willing to pay?" I don't give advice. I share my experience, strength, and hope. When these sorts of things are going on, I try to get them into active service.

MARGE: It really doesn't matter to me what anybody does. I have gotten myself into a position to become an emotional baby-sitter for people when they've insisted on relationships. Relationships take a lot of energy and force you to work your program. If your willing to do that, fine. Then, I've come to the point where I throw the steps back at people, instead of armchair psychology. If they're not willing to participate in that, they just simply have the relationship by themselves, which is fine by me.

MARIASHA: I think it's really individual. I would never tell somebody they can't be in a relationship, and if they choose to be involved in a relationship and choose to pursue it, and problems come up, I would point those things out. I would try to help make that connection. I would certainly try to point out that you want to decrease your stressors, not increase them, and that there seems to be a correlation between your relationship problems and your serenity and spirituality. But I don't believe in shaming. I don't believe in giving ultimatums. I'm not going to threaten somebody that I'm going to withhold my love and support because they are not going to do it my way. If they were engaging in behavior that comprised my integrity, I might need to pull back and say, "I can't be a part of this because I think it's destructive."

I was in a relationship early in recovery. I came into the program in a relationship. I'm still married, thirteen years later, to the same person. If somebody had said to me, "You need to leave your boyfriend, because you're in a relationship and new in recovery," I'm not sure I would've stayed in the fellowship. I was a package deal when I came in. I wouldn't encourage somebody to pound the pavement to find a relationship early in recovery. But again, I wouldn't make any threats to them.

Bob B.: I'd tell him, "Go for it." I don't tell him not to. I tell him the dangers; I tell him what the pitfalls are, because very often we are so new, that we want anybody in our lives to serve as some comfort. I warn him not to get so involved he can't work the program. I don't care what happens in the relationship as long as he is working at recovery. I suggest he'd do well to look at and be prepared for hassles that might occur. It's not that having a relationship is the problem. Many of us have many relationships, but we hadn't had one clean. That's a whole adventure by itself. You learn about you and other people, about attitudes, and about all these feelings that you thought you knew something about, but you find out you don't know anything about them, because you did not experience these feelings.

Leigh: Relationships snag because we don't have the tools to deal with them. Don't make any changes in the first year.

J.P.: I believe there are no victims, only volunteers. What I don't recommend is newcomers together in early recovery. I tell them, "If one male in fifty stays clean and one woman in thirty, what are the odds of both of them being you?" So, if you can avoid it, I think it's a good idea.

JEANETTE: My first rule is not to get involved in my sponsees' personal relationships and whether they should go out with someone or breakup with someone they're already involved with. I will discuss any aspect they want to discuss with me, but I won't get involved in actual decision making unless there is physical abuse. I don't want them saying, "My sponsor said . . ."

GUIDANCE ON STEALING.

LISA: They need to do a Fourth Step or they will continue to do the same behavior.

BEA: She should go to her boss and tell him. And she should be willing to make the amends and take the consequences.

BOB B.: I ask him how he feels about this stealing. Evidently, he must not be feeling too good because he is talking about it. There are many things that go with stealing. I think part of it is rationalizing or justifying stealing. I think one thing that happens as we recover is there's a certain discomfort about our actions that we don't want to live with. That's where the action comes in. You find yourself in one of those situations where the very act of stealing makes you physically uncomfortable: your stomach is flip-flopping and turning upside down, you start breathing hard and everything else, just like the police are chasing you down the street. If you don't want to feel that, you are going to have to stop doing something. Sometimes that's part of the thing, to get you started in action. It's not what somebody else does. Your own feelings will dictate that you do something about it.

J.P.: I stole cassettes out of cars. It haunted me for a long time. I would see cassettes that were big as refrigerators. I was in a lot of pain over it. I tell my sponsees: You can stop stealing right now and go through some pain or stop when the legal system catches you. My suggestion is stop right now and go through some pain.

ED: I love stealing things. I don't anymore, but the urge to get something for nothing is still there. I remind sponsees that everything is a gift, that everything we have is on loan, that even though our mind is telling us we won't be taken care of, our hearts will tell us we will. Listen to your heart. And I point to the First Step, which introduces us to honesty. Be faithful to the truth, to reality, to the universe.

Don't take that. It's not yours.

CHARLES: I've had stealing issues before I got sober. I haven't had them since. My sponsees have. I have a sponsee that's been arrested for stealing since he was sober. It actually had nothing to do with actual stealing, it had to do with his sexual issues. Recently he's gotten himself into dealing with those sexual issues, and he's writing about those and going to groups about it. He's working it out, and he's sober not just in AA rooms, but outside of the rooms as well. Some of the anger's gone. To deal with it, I'd dropped him off at several places, at several meetings, until he finally found the meeting where the solution came out. It wasn't in me. It wasn't in him; it was in the meetings; it was in others. God works through others. By hearing it from others, he could hear himself.

SUZANNE: Don't do it. And if you do, return it, make amends, and take responsibility.

Chapter Nine

Learning From Others

"*I judge less. It's not my job and it gives me a headache.*"

— E D

Answers to the questions: What mistakes have you made as a sponsor, and how have they affected your sponsorship today? How has your style changed? What things do you do now that you didn't use to do?

In recovery, we learn from others' experience; this is the basis of sponsorship. In the first part of this chapter we find out what mistakes our sponsors made that may come up for you— pitfalls you can avoid by learning from their experience. The second part of the chapter focuses on how our sponsors have changed over the years and the things they've learned to do now, with more experience under their belt, that they didn't do early on. Some of what they say will confirm what you already know, and other things will be eye opening. Let them sponsor you here to avoid some of the mistakes that can be made.

WHAT MISTAKES HAVE YOU MADE AS A SPONSOR, AND HOW HAVE THEY AFFECTED YOUR SPONSORSHIP TODAY?

JEANETTE: I used to move them into my house if they didn't have a place to live when I started sponsoring them. There was one gal who was living with me who missed her boyfriend, so I moved him in too. I've learned: Don't feed 'em; teach 'em how to fish. And also don't let them move in.

PATRICE: Being abusive, unforgiving, and taking their behavior personally. I said it before, but it bears repeating: Do not take their behavior personally. It has very little to do with me and a lot to do with them and their disease.

SUZANNE: I think the biggest mistake I've made has been taking on a couple of newcomers at the same time. That was a lot for my schedule. I think sponsoring one new person at a time is enough, because newcomers need a lot of energy and a lot of attention. I don't mind having a newcomer, and then maybe taking on one or two people who have five or eight years of sobriety, who are really along the road. I think it's a big mistake that some people are sponsoring twenty-five newcomers. That's an ego-driven, misrepresentation of helping people, a distorted sense of how you help people. I don't think it's very helpful. I think that's the biggest mistake I've made, that I haven't really been able to fully be there for someone the way she really needed me.

ED: I tried to fix people. I thought I had to have an answer or a comment for everything, and not just any old comment but a profound, earth-shaking comment, a phrase that would turn their lives around. And I didn't. I gave advice where I shouldn't have; I tried to run my sponsees' lives. No good.

LEIGH: Sponsoring friends.

LOIS: The main mistake I feel I made as a sponsor was lending money a couple of times. The results were always disastrous and most times lead to the breakup of the sponsor-sponsee relationship. My sponsor has since directed me not to do this.

M.T.: I had a bad experience when I borrowed money from a sponsee, and I would never do that again.

Also, I start out my sponsees with good structure, suggesting they attend a women's meeting, a step meeting, and a *Big Book* meeting every week. But I haven't maintained the constant flow of step work being done, and I do think that's important. I'm sorry I haven't been able to be consistent in meeting with my sponsees. My schedule is such that it prohibits it timewise, regardless of how good my intentions are to make certain meetings each week. I think it's good to see a sponsee once a week or so at a meeting, hear them share, and check in with them.

J.P.: I was afraid someone would say they didn't want me as a sponsor anymore if I called them on their stuff. Now I'm more apt to do so. Also, I'm not a blanket sponsor. I don't do the same thing with every sponsee. I treat some more gently than others.

BEA: I think one of the mistakes I made was taking on too many women, and then feeling like I didn't have enough time. It affected everybody. It didn't just affect the new girl I took on, it affected all my relationships. I don't do that anymore. Now I'm able to say no. Previously, I didn't know how to say no when people asked me to sponsor them. I'm doing them an injustice by taking them on when I don't have the time.

DANNY: I feel like it was a mistake not pushing one of my sponsees to do his inventory sooner. I think it allowed him to coast downhill. I didn't keep him busy with something. I think there needs to be some kind of a project in the early parts of our recovery lives. It seems like the people who go to recovery houses, that want recovery, tend to be more accepting of projects than people who just start in the

rooms. This sponsee resisted some direction. I should've
just really plowed into him. "I want to see some progress
by this date. I want your Fourth Step done in six weeks.
You're going to do your Fifth by this date." If I'd done that,
it might have cleared a lot of stuff in his head and in his
soul, and he might have realized what an addict he really
was.

There's another sponsee that I have a long distance relationship with. I don't see it as any sort of a mistake, but
I wish I could keep in closer contact with him. He doesn't
call very often. He's still clean; he's going to school; he's
getting his high school degree. But we don't have real contact. He's got somebody out there he talks to, but I'm hop-
ing when he moves back to this side of town, we reestablish
a connection. I don't feel like I've let him down, but I feel
like I tend to get too involved with things and people at
hand. He hasn't called me, so I feel like I should've called
him.

MARIASHA: I don't know whether it's a mistake,
but it's not always pretty to show that you're human,
and I've shown that. I haven't been as available as I
would've liked to have been. There was a time I lost a
baby, and I told the people that I was sponsoring that I
wasn't going to be available much, and the quality of
what I might have to offer could seriously be in question
because of my situation. I gave them the choice to bear
with me or to make whatever changes they felt they
needed to. The same thing happened when I was preg-
nant with Asha. I probably let go of three quarters of all
of the people that I sponsored. I don't know that it was
a mistake. I think it was honoring my own limitations,
including my energy, when I felt I needed to, and recognizing that I couldn't be all things to all people. Part of
me says I should be perfect in all things. I feel like

maybe that was a mistake, maybe I was being selfish. But, I felt like I wanted to give quality recovery to those I was working with. It wasn't a numbers game. It was about quality.

The only other thing that comes to my mind is one particular sponsee who told me she thought I wasn't always as nice to her as she needed me to be. She had a lot of problems, a lot of long-standing family issues, which constantly got in the way of her recovery. So, I would repeatedly say the same things over and over, and she was not able to receive them. I'm sure, from time to time, my direction and tone of voice were difficult for her to receive. So, I think that's a mistake. It's an example of me being human, not being as sensitive or compassionate as an addict in pain might need me to be.

BOB B.: Mistakes . . . everybody makes them. A sponsor is part of the human condition.

I think one of my biggest mistakes was sponsoring women for the wrong reason. They wanted me to sponsor them for the wrong reason, and I wanted to sponsor them for the wrong reason. It usually becomes very chaotic in terms of saying it's not a sponsorship relationship, it is a relationship relationship. So I've learned, for those particular reasons, that I have to really look at those types of sponsorship and those situations. Very often in male/male relationships the same thing occurs. One party is trying to have a different type of relationship than a sponsorship relationship. Very often, people who are looking for sponsors are really looking for fathers, mothers, keepers, employment aides, transportation aides, money, etc. They look for all those things for the wrong reason. You need to become aware that that may be what's happening, that it's not a sponsorship relationship. There are times I thought these were temporary situations, that they would go away, only to find out they didn't go away, only deepened. They didn't just fade away. Regardless of how temporary it was going to be, it became traumatic, so to speak.

CHARLES: What mistakes have I made? I don't think there are any mistakes. I learned that I shouldn't listen to others when they suggest things, even though they may be psychologists or whatever, that I should take it from my Higher Power, and I should meditate on it and let the answer come from within me for what I should do when it comes to those issues with my sponsees, and not take other people's ideas and run with them, let it come up. And if it doesn't come up, then you have to say that's what happened and that was God's will. It wasn't mine.

HAS YOUR STYLE CHANGED? IF SO, WHAT THINGS DO YOU DO NOW THAT YOU DIDN'T USE TO DO?

M.T.: My style hasn't really changed. I know more about the steps now, so my sponsorship is more experienced and knowledgeable concerning the steps and human behavior.

For example, I have my sponsees get a really thorough understanding of Steps Six and Seven before letting them go on to Eight. But now I am much more understanding, compassionate, and forgiving of human frailty. Any judgment I had toward relapsers is gone. I've softened; I'm not as tough about the program. I think it's understandably hard for many people to get it and keep it, so I work a little differently with relapsers now.

PATRICE: I'm much more gentle and loving and less judgmental.

SUZANNE: I think it has changed. When I was newly sober, in my first three or four years, and people would ask me to sponsor them, I felt very, very anxious and uptight about sponsoring them. I felt I had to do it perfectly, and, if I didn't do it right and they drank, it was going to be my fault. Now, I will offer myself as a sponsor if I think people need help and support. But I usually say I'd like to help them as a temporary sponsor, and then if they find someone else, it's perfectly fine. I think I'm much more relaxed about it. I think I have much more compassion and understanding about how difficult it is to get sober. I don't feel the kind of disappointment I used to if people go out. I also don't take it personally. I think my attitude about it is really different.

ED: Sometimes I sponsor my sponsees; sometimes they sponsor me. Sometimes I call up my sponsor and ask him how he's doing. He tells me in detail. And I listen. Sometimes my sponsees call me up and ask how I'm doing. I tell them in detail. And they listen. In the beginning I thought I had to place my sponsor above me. When he turned out to be human, I felt betrayed. Now I know we're all just human beings struggling to get through the day. Sometimes we do it with the greatest of ease. Sometimes we don't.

I listen more. I still like the sound of my own voice, and find myself drifting into preacher mode, but I try to watch for that. Rather than tell them what to do, I've been trying to help them work it out, to find the answers to their problems within their own hearts.

I theorize and pontificate less, meaning I'm more down to earth. Rather than giving my theory, my philosophical take on how something relates to my world view, I try to give concrete examples of how I've worked one or more of the steps to solve a problem.

I judge less. It's not my job and it gives me a headache.

I'm more step oriented. My sponsor really, really believes in NA and in the steps. And I've come to see the wisdom in that. When I first got clean, there was this long period where I had no values. My old values no longer worked, and when I stopped using, I was left with nothing, just vague hints of morals and ethics from Catholic school, concepts that I had abandoned long ago. I had nothing. I replaced them with a home grown philosophy, which though intellectually stimulating, gave me no clear idea of how I should behave on a day-to-day basis. My philosophy had nothing to do with being human, with being with other people. It was really just another way of using, of hiding from myself. The steps introduced me to specific spiritual principles that I could apply in my everyday life. They gave me back my life, let me touch my life without fear.

CHARLES: Everything changes. Everything is different all the time. I have more confidence now than in the beginning.

LEIGH: Now, I am willing to terminate a relationship if the sponsee's behavior is not sincere. I am willing not to sponsor. I wanted the validation of being a sponsor as an ego thing. I believe people should honestly take the time they need for their own recovery before they sponsor others; otherwise, they give the disease away.

BEA: I think if there's anything I've learned or that's changed, it's that I have more of a capacity for compassion and patience. I understand more of addiction, so I try to offer whomever I'm sponsoring what they need, what I think they need. That's really what it comes down to: what they show me is what I'm giving of myself.

DANNY: It's changed a little bit. I think in the beginning I was trying so hard to be accepted as a sponsor, that I was really easy. I'm being a little more assertive with my sponsees, in terms of what I expect of them and what they need to do with direct situations, like sharing. I don't feel they won't like me if I tell them they need to do something. The first sponsee is always the scariest one. It's like, "Oh God, what'll I do?" I think that's probably the biggest change; I'm more assertive in terms of not only telling them what I expect from them, but making sure they do those things, as well as offering them some solutions in the literature.

DON: My ego used to be wrapped up in whether or not my sponsees stayed clean. It's not anymore. It used to be they had to stay clean because their sobriety reflected well on me. I ended up with lots of drunken babies (sponsees). Now I'm a good sponsor either way. I tell the newcomers, when they ask me to sponsor them, that if they think they need a lot of time that I'm very busy and they deserve quality time. They'll wind up with a resentment if I sponsor them, but as an AA member, they can call me anytime. "Here's my number." I've learned through years of experience that this is the best thing to do. It was an ego thing in the beginning. I thought, "How fabulous. You want me to sponsor you." Then I was a sponsor in name only. I picked five sponsors because they were cute.

Someone finally said to me, "Find someone who will talk to you." And I did.

BOB B.: Probably second thoughts about a number of things. I might direct something today, and redirect it tomorrow. If I see a different direction to go in, or if I sent a sponsee to the wrong person, I may try to correct that direction by saying, "That's wrong. You need to go check this person out," or "I gave you some bad information. You need to go do this here." Very often, sponsors like to be right about everything or be the mother, father, confidant, etc., but they're not capable or qualified. Sometimes we don't think about it until after the fact. We have to learn how to stand up and say "I goofed," and take care of the goof, redirect, readvise, or whatever may be needed. I give some bad advice. Very often this bad advice is advice that I've taken myself. I didn't know it was bad. I thought it was good advice. Then I think about it again and say, "Wait a minute, that's what got me into this mess. I better retract that one. Let me go back here and check this out." My character defects show up as often as anybody else's. I make the same mistake over again, but I usually think I altered them in some way, with a different attitude, different perspective, etc.

I guess the style changes have been that I'm not as available as I used to be, that I no longer feel I have to have an answer for every question that comes up, and that I'm not as controlling. Sometimes that's the only way sponsees learn, by acting on their own. Sometimes you just tell them, "No, that's your decision. You need to make that decision." I no longer run out and rescue. One of the roles I played for a lot of years was "Bob to the rescue." I was like, "Let Bob fix it for you. You don't have to. Just let me know what it is, and I'll fix it for you." Very often that was to my own detriment. I ended up, in some ways, feeling the pain of that action. That was part of my character, so I had to deal with it.

MARGE: People go if they're not sincere. My style is simply me and God, however good I'm able to do that on any given day. The principles I believed in are the same. Because of Sara's (my sponsor) emotional honesty, I've been able to be more emotionally honest with people and to vent my own stuff, the kinds of things that I wasn't capable of in the beginning. I was Miss AA. I think that happens with everybody. I don't really think that I have a style. It's just whatever comes out of the mouth or the heart. I try to do it from the heart, which is sometimes hard.

The thing I do differently now is I set firmer boundaries of what I expect. I set firmer boundaries of how closely people stay in touch, if they really mean it. The only reason I started to set them was because I developed and could set boundaries. I didn't have any to begin with. I did a lot of rescuing my first five years, and I took it to an extreme. It's just like anything else: you can't give away what you don't have, and I didn't have the ability early on. So, whatever I have learned is valuable. I don't hold it back from people, because I think we absorb whatever we can handle anyway and everything needs to be repeated; it had to be repeated to me. So, I just trust that process.

Chapter Ten

Some Other Common Issues That May Arise

"Some sponsors think if a sponsee relapses, they are at fault. That means they're responsible for that person staying clean."

— LEIGH

Is it a sponsor's responsibility to stick with a sponsee no matter what? If not, where do you draw the line? What do you do if your sponsee is not working a program? Ways to handle a sponsee's relapse.

....

Sponsees come to us for help, but they aren't always willing to take what they've asked for. They can be (and are almost by definition) scattered, unwilling, irresponsible, and sometimes just annoying. Are sponsors supposed to stick with their sponsees once the commitment has been made? If not, what is fair criteria for breaking the verbal contract to sponsor? Is it enough if you just don't feel like it's going anywhere or does something dramatic need to take place?

So, you've given good direction and your sponsee isn't taking it or is taking a really long time to take action on it . . . it's hard enough to stay clean, sober, abstinent, etc. when you are working a program (and the odds are slim enough then). What do you do if sponsees are not working one?

Relapse is common. But what do you do, as a sponsor, when it occurs? Here are some thoughts from these sponsors' experiences.

IS IT A SPONSOR'S RESPONSIBILITY TO STICK WITH A SPONSEE NO MATTER WHAT? IF NOT, WHERE DO YOU DRAW THE LINE?

M.T.: Not only do I think that you don't stick with them no matter what, I think if they're heading for a relapse and won't take suggestions, that's enough to say sayonara. This is all about willingness to participate in your own recovery. If you're not willing to do the work, why should your sponsor? My time is valuable. If I can't take on new sponsees because I'm already committed to sponsees who are not working a program, I'm not being of service to anyone. Really, I'm being of *disservice* to the newcomer who might benefit from my help but who I have to turn down because I have too many sponsees.

But, on the other hand, if they are doing their best, showing up, writing, taking direction but having problems—yes, I will continue to work with them and see them through till it takes.

SUNNY: I've never fired anyone. I think it is the ultimate rejection. This doesn't mean that I'll work closely with the person, but I don't fire them. I had one sponsee who was drinking but I remained her sponsor.

KAREN: I'll stick with a sponsee as long as I feel it is benefiting her, regardless of relapse. If I believe relapses are recurring because she doesn't really want to get clean or sober or if she says she does want to get clean or sober but will not do the work, I will drop her.

JEANETTE: I feel that I shouldn't have to harass and hound them to stay clean or to do the steps. I'll release them if we're not going anywhere and they're not working the steps. There is a point at which you're no longer useful and you're playing a game. They're constantly in a crisis, in a state of uproar. I don't have the time for that anymore. Now I tell them to call me only at certain hours.

ED: I'm looking for someone to work the steps with. If they don't want to work the steps, they don't need a sponsor. It's very easy to get stuck in the problem. I was stuck there for over twenty years. But that's not what we're about, that's not why we come together. We come together to help each other change. Where there's no change, there's no recovery. So, if they don't want to work the steps, I don't judge them. One choice is just as valid as the next. But I can't let them go on pretending they have a sponsor. I have to break off the relationship.

SUZANNE: Absolutely not. I sponsor people for fun and for free. If people aren't willing to take suggestions, if they're not willing to do what it takes to be sober, it's certainly their choice, but I have a choice about how I want to spend my time, and I chose not to waste it with people who aren't willing to do what it takes to be sober. So, I draw the line based on what people say versus their behavior and their actions. If people can't get into action, if they're just wanting to suck energy and constantly use me as a place to dump their big, sad, negative dramas, I'm not interested. So, I'll tell them I think they need to look for someone else because, clearly, the way I got sober isn't the way they want to get sober, and I can only share with them how I've gotten sober. I only know how to coach people in terms of what worked for me. Often times people aren't willing to do that, so I carry the message, not the person. I don't give people money; I don't let them crash at my house; I don't let them waste a lot of my time. They need to be in action.

LEIGH: No. We're not dumping grounds. Carry the message not the addict. I cannot carry and be around someone who is going to abuse me. I had a sponsee who was screaming and hung up on me. I don't want anyone who is going to scream at me. A friend outside the program said I should not have sponsored her. I draw the line with abuse. My purpose is to help them get through the steps. The selfish and egotistical attitude is that we sponsor for our own recovery. I believe we are sponsoring for their recovery not ours. That is the healthier approach.

NATALIE: I stick with newcomers if they show a desire for thirty days. Even if they slack off and make excuses, I've never told anyone I've sponsored that I didn't want to sponsor them. I've never thrown a baby (sponsee) away.

BEA: I feel that it's my responsibility to stick with a sponsee as long as I believe she wants recovery. As long as she keeps her commitment. I told one girl three times that I didn't think I could sponsor her. One time she was just very, very needy; it was a period. I went to my sponsor and talked to her about it. My sponsor told me that I am there to help this woman change, so I needed to stay with her and help her change. That is my responsibility. So we went back again. Then a couple of times she didn't keep her appointments with me. She went out on a date, but she was really honest about it, saying, "I screwed up." She didn't try to cover it up or rationalize. I told her, "I can't do this, because I don't have a lot of time. I'm willing to work with you, but not like this." She felt really bad. I'm still working with her; it's been about ten months now, and she's coming up on two years soon. I guess I'll continue to, until she doesn't want to be clean, until she's not doing what she needs to do to stay clean. I don't believe it's my responsibility no matter what, but as long as I see that this person has a desire for recovery, I'll hang in there, even when I don't want to.

When there's someone that I'm not real comfortable with, I will try and sponsor them anyway, because I think there's something there for me to learn or grow from. The only time that I've ever said no was when I didn't physically have the time to make the space. Otherwise, even when I haven't wanted to, I've always said yes.

MARIASHA: I don't feel it's my responsibility. If somebody were to relapse and to express a desire to continue to work with me, I would. As far as where I draw the line, I think that would be when we both conclude that everything we've tried still wasn't working. We have to honor the fact that we're not getting along, not connecting or not communicating effectively or they're not happy. Generally, it comes from them. I have never fired a sponsee. And I have never said, "Your behavior is unacceptable to me. I'm not willing to work with you. I don't like your personality," or "I don't like your performance," or "I don't like your attitude." I've never had to say anything like that; I've not been in that situation. I have been in a situation where I have supported the decision of the sponsee when she wasn't content with what she was receiving. And I've supported sponsees in their decision to pursue recovery through other women in the program and to call me if they so chose.

J.P.: Yes. No matter what. There's no vocabulary in the program for dropping or firing. I sponsor people I can't stand! I myself said "Screw that Ninth Step—I'll never do it," and ended up doing one because society exacted it from me, through creditors and people who forced me to make amends. If they say they won't work a step, I have the faith to know that's how they feel today and they'll move on. Work progresses on blind faith. I think it's important that in the selection process we select someone we are able to respect. I did my sponsor selection by drug used. That way, we endeared ourselves to each other in early recovery.

WHAT DO YOU DO IF YOUR SPONSEE ISN'T WORKING A PROGRAM?

M. T.: This is the question that started this book. This seemed to be my constant dilemma. I had bright, clean sponsees who started out with half the program I started out with as a newcomer and they didn't improve—it only got worse around Step Four, and again at Six, Seven and Eight. They're not relapsing, but they're not changing, either; they're just coasting. What do you do to motivate them? Does it not matter if they don't work a program? I still don't have an answer. These will be some of the questions in the next book! I think, honestly, cut them loose if they won't do the work, relapse or not.

JEANETTE: I had one sponsee I was giving a lot of advice, and she wouldn't do a single thing I asked. I said, "I'm not doing you any good; this is not working." I fired her. I also said, "I'm still your friend." I will go quite a ways with someone, but once I've reached a certain point, it's over. You need to decide whether or not you're doing the person any good.

PATRICE: It's my place to point out their behavior and let them know they will have to pay the price for that behavior. And, then to see what direction they will take. If they want support, they will come to me. I will work with them at whatever level they are on. If they want a sponsor in name only, I let them know I'm aware of this, but beyond that, it's not my call; it's theirs.

BEA: I tell them they have to get another sponsor, because I can only give them what was given to me. If they're not going to do what I did, they need somebody else. I've done that before. It turned out that was the motivation the woman needed to change.

DANNY: It depends a lot on the individual. For example, one of my sponsees had reached three years. About three or four months after that, he stopped coming to the regular meetings he was going to. He kept one of his commitments, which didn't require leaving his home. But he just failed to show up. He'd call me once a week, and we'd talk. I'd say, "What's happening?" And he'd go through all these, "I'm feeling this, and I'm feeling depressed. I can't beat this. If I could get out of this isolation . . ." I'd say, "You know what the answer to that is." He'd reply, "I know. I need to get out, go to meetings, and do stuff." It would be that same conversation week after week, until he stopped calling.

Before this happened we had some real deep, intense conversations about the patterns of relapse. We had a real good friend who had seven years and relapsed. We had discussed the signs. Every time, it was the same signs, the same things they didn't do. So, here he was doing those things that we had talked about.

After about three weeks, he calls me up one day and we talk. He says, "Oh, by the way, I went out Friday night." I said, "I'm not surprised. Tell me about it." It was the same scenario: he went out to dinner with some business associates who were not in the program. They had a drink. So he had a couple of drinks with them. I told him, "You made a conscious decision to put something in your body that you knew could change your mood." I just left him to his own thoughts. I threw things out that he knew were true. I just let it go. I can't make him go to meetings.

When sponsees do something that I suggest they don't

do, or they don't follow a suggestion, I just do the old "I told you so." I tell them, "We talked about this, and you know better. This is life on life's terms. You take the wrong path, you pay the price." I don't get angry with them; I know that's not going to help them. It's real important to remain compassionate.

I had another sponsee who was struggling with his program. His behavior wasn't helping his recovery. I told him, "You know I don't approve of this and neither does the book. It's not just me, it's the concept. It's something based on experience." He finally let it go. But, it was something he was so used to doing; he had to make a surrender and let go. This was a drug for him.

DON: If they won't work the program, I don't have a lot of time for them. I might read them, tell them off. I let them know when they're working the steps it solves problems. Some people are rocketed into sobriety.

MARGE: I draw the line a lot more clearly now that I've been sober longer. I used to think that the old timers in AA were very harsh, unloving, and strict, and really deprived people of recovery by their attitude. I no longer think that way. What's worked for me is love. I like that approach. However, I draw the line if someone is not working her program. When someone drinks or uses, I'm there for her, but I also ask her to examine what happened, why she was not willing to do whatever it was. Did she not do a good first, second, and third step? What happened? And does she really want to be sober? I think we force sobriety on people who do not want it. I mean sobriety is not only physically not drinking or using, it's a state of being. And, unless you achieve that state of being, you're merely dry and abstinent. Bill W., the founder of AA, says that any program based on mere abstinence is doomed to failure. I believe that. So encouraging people to come to AA meetings between drinks is depriving them of the wonder that can be in their lives.

CHARLES: What do I do if they're not working the program? I slowly remind them, in a general way or sometimes in a more specific way, that recovery is a commitment with themselves. I tell them the only thing they have to do is pick up the phone and get back into a meeting. Usually, we're not working the program because we're out of commitment with ourselves. It's so easy. Again, all you have to do is pick up the phone and start again. We forget that's how easy it is, we think of it as being difficult. I think that's why it's so important we learn how to use the phone in the beginning, to call people, to tell people what's going on. If we're not working a program, we're into our heads. And as long as we're in our heads, we're not out there; we're out to destroy ourselves.

MARIASHA: I point it out to them. I've said this earlier: I believe there's a correlation between your emotional well-being and the program you're working. If a sponsee is really crazy, driven, obsessed, angry, hostile, and acting out, I would say, "What do you think the character defect is that's going on? When's the last time you worked the sixth and seventh steps? When's the last time you really surrendered and put your role in your life under the care of God? Where do you stand with that? What's going on?" If they're not working a program, I think it's important for me to give them my perception: "I haven't seen you in a meeting in quite a while. I'm just wondering what's going on? Have you been to meetings?" Or try, in a nonconfrontational way, to point out my observations. Then they have to make their ultimate choices. Sometimes, if you can express it in

a loving way, it can be a breakthrough. That's when somebody can surrender and acknowledge that they've really hit
bottom, let out steam. That may allow them to start over.

What I try to do is love and support somebody that's not
working a program. But I also maintain my boundaries. I
feel when I compromise my integrity, or put myself into
situations that could be threatening for me, I jeopardized
my own recovery. If somebody wants to meet me at a meeting or just meet, I'm willing to do that. But I'm not willing
to go down where somebody is practicing their disease and
do a 12-step call on them. I think maintaining boundaries is
important in that regard. I just try to be loving and supportive and invite them to participate in recovery with me
whenever they feel they can.

BOB B.: If they're not working a program, shame on
them. They are not doing the things I suggested. I say,
"What did you expect? I can't do it for you." So if you're
not doing it, don't expect anything different from what you
get. You stopped using, but you can get unmanageable.

WAYS TO HANDLE A SPONSEE'S RELAPSE.

SUZANNE: I tell people to have faith and not to give up,
not to shame themselves about it, to get back to meetings,
raise their hands, and participate. This is a deadly disease
and meetings are there for us to get sober. I share with them
that my mother went to meetings for a year, drinking after
every meeting, but she died with eighteen years of sobriety.
I tell them all that's required for membership is a willingness
to stop drinking. I really encourage people to have compassion with themselves and to look into themselves to see what
their degree of willingness is and what their triggers are that
cause the relapse, so they can address those triggers.

CHARLES: I've never really stopped sponsoring anybody because they relapsed. I have somebody who has relapsed maybe three or four times. I feel it's part of his process. I feel his problems are definitely not mine, that my problems are not his. I remember the lessons I learned were very big, that there were people there for me, and that I also relapsed. I tried to stop drinking for three and a half years before I did stop drinking. I remember the people that stood beside me. I can tell you their names, and I can tell you they never saw me sober, never saw me breathe a sober breath, but they were always beside me. I remember that well. So I can't give up anybody.

LEIGH: I ask them, "Do you really want to get clean?" I tell them about people who have died. I thank them for coming back and ask them to write out their relapse, to keep it and read it when they feel like getting high. Some sponsors think if a sponsee relapses, they are at fault. That means they're responsible for that person staying clean.

NATALIE: If they relapse, I tell them to make ninety meetings in ninety days, sit up front, and take the cotton out of their ears. My mouth was moving my whole first year. I had no business speaking without doing the work. I tell them to take commitments, shake hands—be the greeter at a meeting.

BEA: I try to get them right back into the full swing of the program, into meetings, into connecting again, into not beating themselves up, and into looking at the future, not the past. It's over, it's done, and there's something to be learned from it. I'll have them write about it. I'll have them do Steps One, Two, and Three just on that going out.

DANNY: I think the only basic line that I draw is a "go out and stay out." If they get totally out of touch and unresponsive for a period of time, I'd give them ultimatums. At this point, there's a lot that I'd forgive. I see myself more as a guide than a strict overseer of their recovery. They have to run their own recovery, and I tell them that. I'm there to help them deal with certain things in their lives that I've had experience with, or that I know how to interrupt, but, they have to do what they have to do. If we talk about something being detrimental, and they go and do it anyway, I try to turn it into a lesson. Every time I can, I try to let them see the recovery lesson in what they've done, whether it's good or bad. I'm easy.

DON: It doesn't break my heart if they go out. I expect them to get loaded if they're not following a program. When they say, "What happened?" I say, "You won't do what is suggested." I say, "You are selfish and self-centered." I get hard on them. I point out where they're wrong.

MARGE: I put the decision as to whether they want to be sober on them, totally. I also make it very clear that if they want me to be available, I am, and that there's been no change in our relationship. Usually someone who wants to be sober assures me of that immediately or at least by the next day. I also have had a lot of people who never call me again, and that tells me something. It tells me they're really not committed. This is not hard; the steps are not difficult in that sense of the word, but they're not easy either. They require a lot of commitment, and if you don't have that commitment, I really believe that you're better off drinking.

LISA: I tell them: "Keep doing what you're doing, you'll keep getting what you have." But I have stuck with them more than once.

MARIASHA: I think it's really a very individual situation. I have not had many sponsees that have relapsed. A lot of the people have come to me with time clean. They've already been in the program for many years. I haven't had much experience with relapse.

J.P.: First, I feel like I want to drop the person, which is my ego at work. I think, "No sponsee of mine should be using." I don't condemn or chastise. Do they know what they're doing? Some are chronic, meaning that they find a continued, prolonged abstinence from drugs is no longer desirable. Some think they have a handle on it. That doesn't last too long, and they usually fail to make a program. I love them through it. I say, "Get some sleep and call me in the morning." I tell them, "I'm here for you no matter what happens. You can count on me where you can't count on others." I tell them they can't count on mom and dad, but I'll be there with them at their funeral. They can't count on their wives, but I'll be there with them in divorce court. A sponsor is the one thing you can count on if you believe that he will not judge you and help you go through what you're going through.

LOIS: If they've slipped, I tell them to write about how their powerlessness over their addiction created their going out and to write about how unmanageable their life was out there.

ED: I was a chronic relapser. I couldn't put more than three days together. But I kept coming to meetings because I wanted to get clean. But I didn't want to stop using. I thought you could be clean and use at the same time.

Some people say, "It's about drugs." Other people say, "It's not about drugs." I say, "It's about drugs, and it's not about drugs." It's always about choice. Each day, for some reason, I've chosen not to use. That's how I've managed to remain abstinent. But being clean involves changing everything about my life: the way I think, the way I look at things, the way I listen, the way I talk, the way I walk, the way I sit, the way I breathe. Everything. It means learning how to be a human being. It means learning how to be comfortable in my own skin. It means accepting myself, perhaps coming to believe that I'm okay, just the way I am, and learning how to reflect this in my everyday activity. It means taking responsibility for my life, and this means working the steps. Sometimes it's not just about drugs. But in order to work the steps, I have to stop using.

So I tell them to keep coming. That's all. I try not to judge them for using or for being unable to stop using. They're addicts, that's what they're supposed to do. Each choice is valid. I don't use because I'm lazy. I just don't have the energy to run all of over trying to cop drugs. And my life is so much more manageable now. The first step tells us we're powerless over our addiction and that our life has become hell on earth. We'll always be powerless over our addiction. We'll never be able to control our using. But we can learn how to manage our lives. That's all we can hope for.

SUZANNE: I will have a conversation with them about what I'm noticing. I really do nothing except have a conversation. I believe it's the person's responsibility to work their own program, that I'm just there to assist them.

PATRICE: I go over their relapse patterns. Every relapse holds the tools for total success. It's very important to cover every detail. Nothing is an accident; there's always a clear path to the relapse. The very last step in a relapse is the picking up of the drug or drink. I know specifically how to get drunk and loaded. I need to completely understand how to stay clean and sober. Each relapse takes a lot out of the person's belief that this program will work for them. I feel that addicts and alcoholics are people that believe in magic, and the people who come in and stay sober the first time believe the magic really works for them. But with each relapse, the magic wears thinner and thinner. Their recovery becomes harder and harder. I feel relapses happen at times when new breakthroughs can occur. They're the times when the terror is the greatest. The relationship changes if they continue to drink/use; there's no way it won't, because I'm doing something they can't seemed to do. It puts fear and anger between us; there's nothing I can say or do to take that away. I'm still there for them, but I have to have stronger boundaries so they don't destroy me and my life with their disease.

JEANETTE: I'll keep working with relapsers, keep checking what the cause was. Some are born relapsers. Some are so damaged by the drugs they have no capacity to remember the things that can change their thinking. The ones that die—it breaks your heart and you never get over it.

KAREN: When a sponsee relapses, it always gives me cause to reevaluate her program. My tendency is to suggest she increase what she's already doing: go to more meetings, take more commitments, make more phone calls to other sober women throughout the day, pray more often, do more readings from the books, etc. But I find relapse is less about not working a program, than it is about making a decision. I find that decision is often already made, whether the sponsee realizes it or not, long before she relapses, and therefore, in spite of her words and sometimes her actions, she hasn't made a complete and total surrender. Hopefully it will take only one relapse for her to make that surrender.

Chapter Eleven

Additional Thoughts on Sponsorship

"Anything is possible if you have someone who believes in you. Don't try to beat them down. They've already done that with drugs and alcohol."

— NATALIE

ADDITIONAL THOUGHTS FROM
OUR PARTICIPANTS.

....

....

There were some great responses during the interviews that didn't have a home in any particular chapter. Here are some additional pearls of wisdom from our experienced and caring group of sponsors

Following this chapter I have included a Suggested Reading List and the Step Worksheets.

....

CHARLES: One thing I've always done is to go outside the AA program to find help with problems I've had. I've found a lot of help in the West Hollywood Gay and Lesbian Center. I found they can help you on HIV issues. I'm not HIV+, but some of my sponsees are. I'm going to the seminars with them now, where they deal with those issues, so I know what to say to them. Those are the issues I don't know how to deal with, things I have no experience with. We begin a new relationship; we go out and do things together and deal with these issues together. We both learn at the same time. So my sponsee is really helping me to become more well rounded in the community.

My responsibility to God is to give back whenever asked, what was so freely given to me. This is a gift. It is unmerited, unwarranted and undeserved. I can only give it away the way I got it—from those who are still around.

SUNNY: Listening is an art. My sponsor listens. She told me that I was a controller. I didn't believe it.

I give all the stuff I have available, but sponsees need to find their own way. The goal for me is to do it like the *Big Book* says.

....

JEANETTE: Ten sponsees is my cutoff. My personal responsibilities preclude me from having more. I don't feel I can do that much good for more than that number. Now I can get together with my girls on a pretty regular basis. Luckily, they've never all been in a crisis at the same time.

Sponsees tend to feel like nothing happens and they're not doing well. But all things are possible. If you stay clean, the situation is improved. Remember, you *make* mistakes; you *are not* a mistake.

PATRICE: I no longer have a sponsor; I have a friend. When I need her to be a sponsor I tell her. Sometimes she tells me. I do the same with sponsees. A great sponsee to work with helps a lot and continues to work her own program with her own sponsor's support with a total devotion of improving their lives.

At what point should someone begin to sponsor others? After they've worked the first five steps or even better if they've worked them all.

ED: Working the steps is about coming to believe in yourself, learning to trust yourself, to trust that voice that years ago you stopped listening to because it told you not to use and you couldn't/didn't want to. So we learn how to stop running from ourselves, to sit still and settle into ourselves. We learn how to breathe.

LOIS: I definitely think people with a long clean time need sponsors. I just don't think they use them as frequently as in the early days. I have had the same sponsor for fourteen years (she has twenty years) and it has been great because she knows exactly how I have changed.

I feel the most awful thing a sponsor can do to a sponsee (short of the usual, like sleeping with them or using with them) is not to return phone calls promptly. When I sign up as a sponsor, I promise in my heart to be available for the sponsee's needs, by phone or in person, and to practice loving them as they are, and to listen for anything coming in from my Higher Power with which to make a suggestion to them.

CHARLES: How long I stay with sponsees depends on their willingness. For instance, if they made amends to people and I know they're sort of stopped by some of those amends, I try to look and see what they were stopped by and try to get them going in that area. But if I see they are going through a lot of things and need to process for awhile, I let them have that time. I'm not pushy on steps. I know they're dealing with it in their own way. I've learned I'm not God with my sponsees in those steps, and I can't pound the steps into them. But, if I see them struggling over the same thing for maybe three or four months, sometimes I just let them struggle. I think it's good for them.

I say that if you do as we (the other people I sponsor and the other people who belong to the different groups I belong to) do, you will stay sober. I believe if you don't do what we do, you'll get drunk again. If you have a strong sobriety, I think you will always have a strong sponsorship. If you see someone who has good sobriety, you'll see good sponsorship. I don't think there's a question about it.

LEIGH: Sponsorship should be mandatory.

If you share for more than five minutes, you need to talk to your sponsor.

I've spoken at meetings in Turkey, France, England, and all over Europe and found that the way you did your drugs is the way you do your program.

MARGE: There seems to be a syndrome that happens to everyone: the sponsor is admired as the greatest thing since sliced bread, the "know all." I try to make sure my sponsees know I am not the answer, instead that God is the answer. I don't encourage them to ask six people every time they have a nose twitch in order to get six different opinions to chose from, but I encourage them to be interested in other people's programs.

NATALIE: Some sponsees don't need tough love. Sometimes the gentler way is more effective. I believe in honesty. Anything is possible if you have someone who believes in you. Don't try to beat them down. They've already done that with drugs and alcohol.

DANNY: I've been married for a long time, and everybody that I sponsor is single. Sometimes it's taxing when we get into certain areas, like relationships. There are things that make relationships work. They don't "just happen." Sometimes, when I try to pass that on to someone who is younger and single, he doesn't really want to believe it. So, all I can do is offer some common sense without being pushy. There are certain basic relationship principles that you can take from this program and transfer to an existing relationship and they change it—they absolutely change it.

One of the biggest gifts of my recovery is sponsoring. I like to pass stuff on. This is a chance to pass it on, a chance to stay in touch with a part I sometimes feel like I've grown away from. I'm constantly reminded of things I've done, by listening to my sponsees talk about things they remember or things they just did.

Relative to the things I ask sponsees to do, if I'm going

to sponsor them, they have to understand that I go to Narcotics Anonymous. I'm a member of this fellowship only, and that's what I expect them to do. They need to read the *Basic Text*, go to NA meetings, and use certain language. That's it. Some of them have gone to all the different meetings when they were in recovery houses, so they speak all the different languages. It's a hard habit to break, but it's important that somebody has one fellowship and their sponsor is in that same fellowship, and they do all the business in one house. It avoids confusion and avoids excuses and denial. I let them know this is where I got clean, and, if they want me to work with them, this is what they have to do.

DON: Sponsees don't require as much time when they get time. After they've grown up I tell them, "Now you go back and sponsor."

I think the idea of perfection is a disservice. We're not Christian missionaries. We've been really crazy. I'm much more compassionate and tolerant recognizing that people are trying to make it. I try to help them and love them and have fun doing it. In this program you can make it, even if you are a fool.

MARIASHA: My sponsor has told me there were times in her recovery she called her sponsor every week. She was in a relationship and was struggling. My sponsor is in a fairly stable place in her life right now. For the past year or so a year she hasn't seen her sponsor. I think relationships wax and wane. I have one sponsee I've worked with since she was clean. She's got eight years now and probably calls once every two weeks just to check in. I have other people who call only when they have a need. There were times when I have called my sponsor and said, "I realize a long time has passed and maybe my relationship with you isn't working. I don't know if it's not working because I'm not working it, making it work, or trying to make it work, or if we're just not a good match." She has said to me, "I don't have any expectation of how often you should call."

I am comforted by knowing there's one person who has known me from the beginning. I have close friends; I have a few people who have been clean as long as I have. I think they know pieces of me. They know what I share with them, but they don't know everything because you don't tell everything about yourself to people you know. We get together, we have dinner, we hang out, we talk about a current issue. But my sponsor heard my inventory. I certainly don't call her every week; I don't see her very often. But recently we decided we want to see more of one another. I think it's as much for her benefit as it is for my benefit. She's got seventeen years clean and there aren't a lot of people that she benefits from. I think it's a reciprocal relationship. She also doesn't have family she sees much of. She enjoys being around my husband and my daughter. It's comforting for her to be in that environment and to spend time with us.

BOB B.: You reach the point of understanding that everything that happens in living is common to living. I think one of an addict's biggest problems or obstacles is some fantasy we have that life is supposed to be "oh so wonderful," in the sense that it should be entertaining rather than work. Things happen living everyday that you have to work on, deal with, or confront. It takes addicts a long time to understand that here it is, that life is what it is. We don't have to run away from it, avoid it, or dismiss it like it's not happening. I think we have to be willing or prepared to accept life as it is and that you're not alone, that you don't have to face it alone. There are going to be some difficulties you'll have to ask for help with. I think it becomes an attitude change that comes about in the process. It doesn't mean there is no pain, difficulty, or feeling attached to it, but that's life too.

I think everybody needs sponsorship. I don't know if anybody comes away freehanded in terms of not needing a sponsor or somebody to confide in, to talk things through with. I have found no one yet who gets by that way. I think it's kind of a transition. We're not self-sufficient on our own. Our condition or illness, addiction, is always present; it's always there. It's like something you dismiss. It's not out to get you. Once we get too far away from it, we start a regression that goes along with that; I call it working the steps from Twelve to One. They call it steps for not being in recovery. So, if you don't want that to happen, you better be doing some maintenance or doing some other things along the way.

I have a number of long-term sponsees. I've had the opportunity to see them grow up, to see the attitude change, to see their responsibility change, to see them mature, to actually see them become adults.

J.P.: Watch out for people with long clean time who are into the Guru syndrome, loose cannons who philosophize and council rather than sponsor. How can you humble yourself before a person with no humility?

That two sponsors stuff—spiritual and step—is nonsense. It just means that you are afraid to invest too much in one person.

SUZANNE: My experience with my own sponsor is that I've outgrown the relationship; we became friends. But I have been growing in ways that she hasn't and vice versa. The reasons why we connected in the beginning no longer exist anymore, and we really don't have enough in common for me to continue the relationship in the same way that I did in the beginning. I'm still friends with her, but I've really been looking around to find somebody else to work with. I feel like I've outgrown her. I think that's also occurred in the people that I've sponsored. Over time, we become friends, but then they've looked other places for other things.

M.T.: Sponsorship is the greatest gift. It brings home the point that we're not alone, that there is one person who has a personal interest in our recovery, who cares if we succeed and don't go back out. I think people (this means me, too) who care about how many sponsees they have, as if that were some measure of their recovery, need to focus on their own program.

You find out what you *don't* have to give when someone asks for it. It's just then that you wish you had it.

Suggested Reading

The **Alcoholics Anonymous** book (the **Big Book**) is the original book written by Bill W., with editorial input from the first one hundred sober alcoholics. It's like the bible to the Twelve Steps, beautifully written, profound and passionate. If you don't have a copy, get one and read it, regardless of what fellowship you belong to. You don't know what you're missing.

Bill's **Twelve Steps and Twelve Traditions** is in the same vein as the *Big Book* and just as enlightening. A really good place to get a full understanding of the steps and the principles they represent.

The **Basic Text** of Narcotics Anonymous is their equivalent of the *AA Big Book* and is tailored to addicts. (It will hit home if you are one.) The **Twelve Steps and Twelve Traditions** is more in-depth and better written than the early original work though.

Twelve Steps and Twelve Traditions of Alanon and the **Overeaters Anonymous** text are excellent resources. Again, you don't need to be in either fellowship to use them. Overeaters Anonymous is famous for its comprehensive analysis of the steps, especially the Fourth.

There are many step guides if you feel you need something with more specific direction. NA has some on the steps. The one for the Fourth Step, if done in its entirety, could take a year to complete. However, it is still a good resource because you can take what you need and leave the rest. Hazelden offers good guides for every step.

I cannot recommend too highly **One Day at a Time in Alanon**. It is great bedside reading. I found out about it from a friend who swears by it, and she isn't even in a program!

Writing
the Steps

STEP PREPARATION

♦ Define and expand on the following concepts:

- • STEPS
- • ABSTINENCE
- • RECOVERY
- • CLEAN
- • SERENITY
- • CHOICE

♦ What are the steps, and what does it mean to "work" the steps?

♦ Do we have to work the steps to stay clean?

♦ What step do we have to work before we can begin to work the steps?

♦ Do we work the steps, or do they work us?

♦ Why are the steps written in the past tense?

♦ What would your life be like if you worked the steps?

♦ How do we know when to move on to the next step?

Step One

- Read about this step in the books on the Suggested Reading list.

- In light of what you've read, define and expand on the following concepts:

    - Admit
    - Power
    - Powerless
    - Unmanageable
    - Control
    - Honesty
    - Surrender
    - Acceptance
    - Choice

- List *all* the things you have power over.

- List *all* the things you are powerless over.

- How was your life unmanageable when you were using, and how is it unmanageable now? Give examples.

- How do you know you are powerless over (fill in your disease)?

- If we can't manage our own lives, does that mean we no longer have the right to make decisions about our life?

- What would your life be like if you admitted your powerlessness?

- Having admitted this, what do we do now?

STEP TWO

♦ Read about this step in the books on the Suggested Reading list.

♦ In light of what you've read, define and expand on the following concepts:

- BECOME
- BELIEVE
- POWER
- RESTORE
- SANITY
- INSANITY
- INHERENT
- OPEN-MINDEDNESS
- FORGIVENESS

♦ What does "come to believe" mean? How does it happen?

♦ What is a power greater than ourselves?

♦ What does "restore us to sanity" mean?

♦ What is being restored, and how long does it take?

♦ What is implied in the idea of restoration?

♦ What would your life be like if you could be restored to sanity?

♦ Having come to believe, what do we do now?

STEP THREE

♦ Read about this step in the books on the Suggested Reading list.

♦ In light of what you've read, define and expand on the following concepts:

- DECISION

- TURN OVER

- LIFE

- WILL

- CARE

- HIGHER POWER

- BODY

- MIND

- FEAR

- LOSS

- WORRY

- WILLINGNESS

♦ Why do we make this decision?

♦ What does "our will and our lives" include?

♦ Is there anything that we *don't* turn over?

♦ What is *your* understanding of God?

♦ What does "I surrender to the will of God" mean?

♦ What would your life be like if you could let go and
let God in?

♦ Having made this decision, what do we do now?

STEP FOUR

♦ Read about this step in the books on the Suggested
Reading list.

♦ In light of what you've read, define and expand on
the following concepts:

- SEARCHING

- FEARLESS

- MORAL

- INVENTORY

- PAST

- PRESENT

- FUTURE

- RESENTMENT

- ANGER

- FEAR

- GARBAGE

- REALITY

- RESPONSIBILITY

♦ Why do we make this searching and fearless inventory?

♦ Are we capable of doing anything fearlessly?

◆ Is there anything that we *don't* list?

◆ What would your life be like if you knew who you were?

◆ Make a fearless and moral inventory.

◆ Having made this inventory, what do we do now?

STEP FIVE

◆ Read about this step in the books on the Suggested Reading list.

◆ In light of what you've read, define and expand on the following concepts:

  • ADMIT

  • EXACT NATURE

  • WRONGS

  • POWERLESS

  • TRUST

◆ Why do we share our inventory with God?

◆ How do we admit something to ourselves?

◆ Why do we share our inventory with another human being?

◆ What kind of human being do we share with?

◆ Why are our assets not a part of this step?

♦ What would your life be like if you no longer feared being found out?

♦ What would your life be like if you could accept who you were?

♦ Having admitted this inventory, what do we do now?

STEP SIX

♦ Read about this step in the books on the Suggested Reading list.

♦ In light of what you've read, define and expand on the following concepts:

- BECOME
- ENTIRELY
- WILLING
- DEFECT
- CHARACTER
- REMOVE
- RESPONSIBILITY

♦ What does "become entirely willing" mean? How does it happen?

♦ What would your life be like if your defects could be removed?

♦ Make a list of your character defects.

♦ Having become willing, what do we do now?

Step Seven

♦ Read about this step in the books on the Suggested Reading list.

♦ In light of what you've read, define and expand on the following concepts:

- Humble
- Remove
- Shortcoming
- Humility
- Human
- Powerless
- Mindfulness

♦ Why do we ask our Higher Power to remove our defects?

♦ What replaces our defects?

♦ Do we need anyone's permission to change?

♦ What would your life be like if you allowed your Higher Power to remove your defects?

♦ Having become humble, what do we do now?

Step Eight

♦ Read about this step in the books on the Suggested Reading list.

- In light of what you've read, define and expand on the following concepts:

  - LIST
  - HARM
  - BECOME
  - WILLING
  - AMENDS
  - ALL
  - DEGREE

- Why do we make this list?

- Is there anyone that we *don't* put on this list?

- There are degrees of harm. Make up a scale or a range.

- Why do we make this list *before* we become willing?

- What would your life be like if you could make all these amends?

- Make a list of the people you have harmed.

- Having become willing, what do we do now?

STEP NINE

- Read about this step in the books on the Suggested Reading list.

- In light of what you've read, define and expand on the following concepts:

  - DIRECT
  - AMENDS

- POSSIBLE

- INJURE

◆ Why do we make these amends?

◆ What does "direct amends" mean?

◆ What does "whenever possible" mean?

◆ Do we need anyone's permission to amend our behavior?

◆ What would your life be like if you made all these amends?

◆ Having begun to make our amends, what do we do now?

STEP TEN

◆ Read about this step in the books on the Suggested Reading list.

◆ In light of what you've read, define and expand on the following concepts:

- CONTINUE

- PERSONAL

- INVENTORY

- WRONG

- PROMPTLY

- ADMIT

♦ Why do we take this inventory?

♦ When do we take this inventory?

♦ What does "promptly admitted" mean?

♦ What would your life be like if you were aware of what you were doing?

♦ What would your life be like if you admitted when you were wrong?

♦ Having accepted responsibility for our actions, what do we do now?

STEP ELEVEN

♦ Read about this step in the books on the Suggested Reading list.

♦ In light of what you've read, define and expand on the following concepts:

- SEEK
- PRAYER
- MEDITATION
- IMPROVE
- CONSCIOUS
- CONTACT
- KNOWLEDGE
- POWER
- ACCEPTANCE
- SERENITY
- SPIRITUAL PATH

◆ What does "conscious contact" mean?

◆ Why do we seek to improve this contact?

◆ Why do we pray only for "knowledge of His will for us"? Why not for things? Why not for *our* will?

◆ What does "I surrender to the will of God" mean?

◆ What would your life be like if you improved your conscious contact?

◆ Having committed ourselves to a spiritual path, what do we do now?

STEP TWELVE

◆ Read about this step in the books on the Suggested Reading list.

◆ In light of what you've read, define and expand on the following concepts:

- SPIRITUAL

- AWAKENING

- RESULT

- MESSAGE

- SUFFERS

- PRACTICE

- PRINCIPLES

- ALL

- AFFAIRS

- FREEDOM
- GRATITUDE
- SERVICE

♦ What is a "spiritual awakening" and when do we have one?

♦ Why is a spiritual awakening needed *before* we can successfully carry the message to the addict who still suffers, *before* we can practice these principles in all our affairs?

♦ What does it mean to drop your "body and mind" into the lap of God?

♦ What would your life be like if you had a spiritual awakening?

♦ What would your life be like if you practiced these principles at all times?

♦ Now that we're awake, what do we do now?

If you have a good sponsor, are a good sponsor, or know a good sponsor who you would recommend as a participant in a sequel to this book, please send that person's name and number to me.

I would also very much like to hear *your* comments on this book or any suggestions you might have for chapter topics in a sequel.

Sincerely,

M. T.
A Sponsorship Guide for Twelve-Step Programs
c/o St. Martin's Press
175 Fifth Avenue
New York, N.Y. 10010